Adult Coloring Book
with
COLOR BY NUMBER or NOT
VOL. 4
MANDALAS (Vol. 2)

By: C. R. Gilbert

Stress Relieving Designs - Excellent For Beginners

Printed by CreateSpace, An Amazon.com company

ISBN-13: 978-1535122382

ISBN-10: 1535122382

How to use this book:

* Get out your pencils or crayons. **Markers WILL BLEED** through so be sure to put some extra paper or a piece of cardboard behind the design you are coloring.

* Find a design you would like to color and go to its swatch page. This page has the colors listed that go with the numbers in the drawing. It also has a couple of test spots on this page to test your own colors. Then pick the numbered or unnumbered version of the design to color. There is a numbered and unnumbered page for each design.

* **All the color names with a corresponding color swatch are printed on the back cover.**

* RELAX & HAVE FUN!!!

* **Please provide a review of this book. I'm always looking for ways to make improvements.**

Please visit our website to get a

FREE

book on Basic Color Theory:

crgilbert.com/free

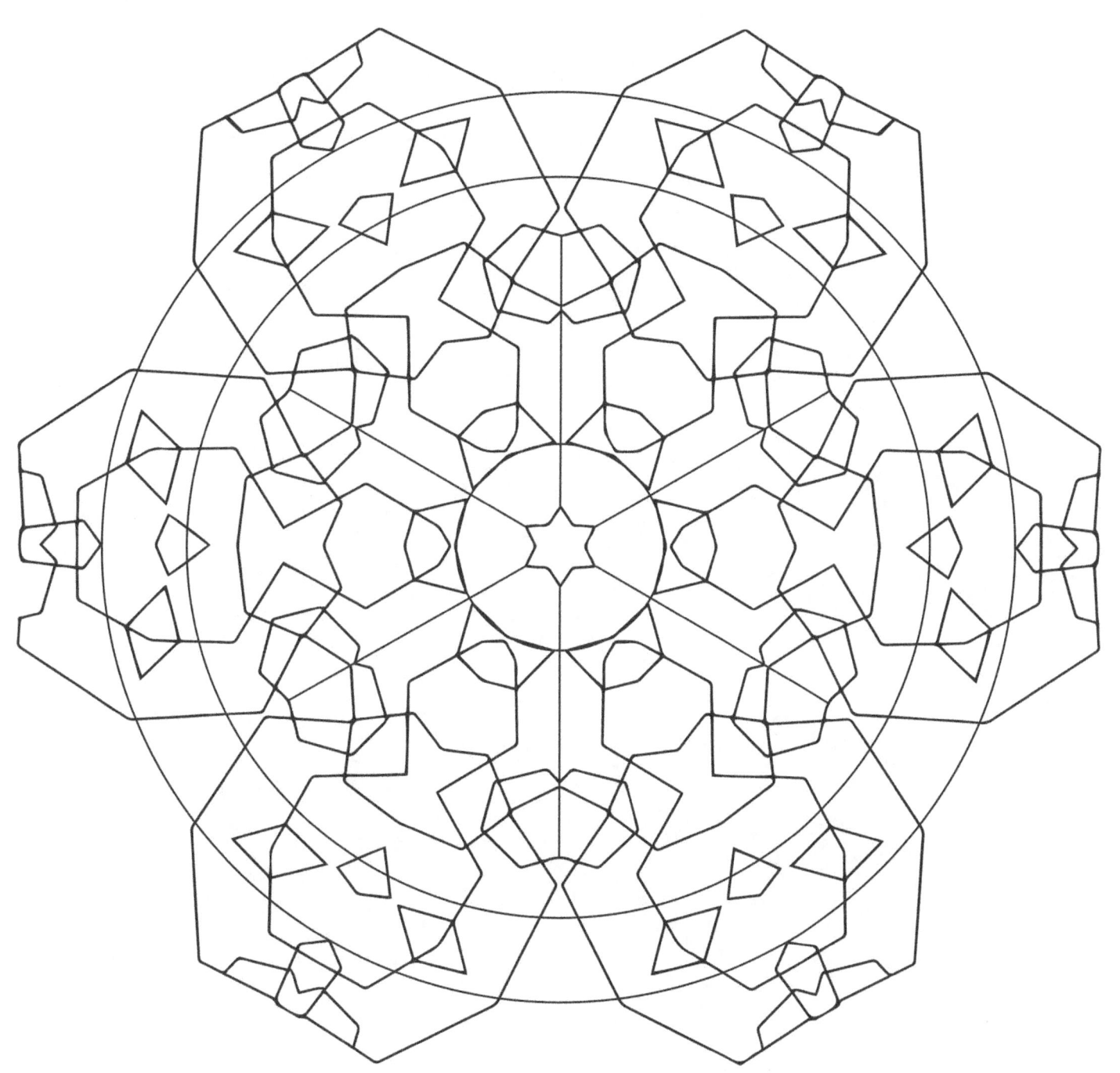

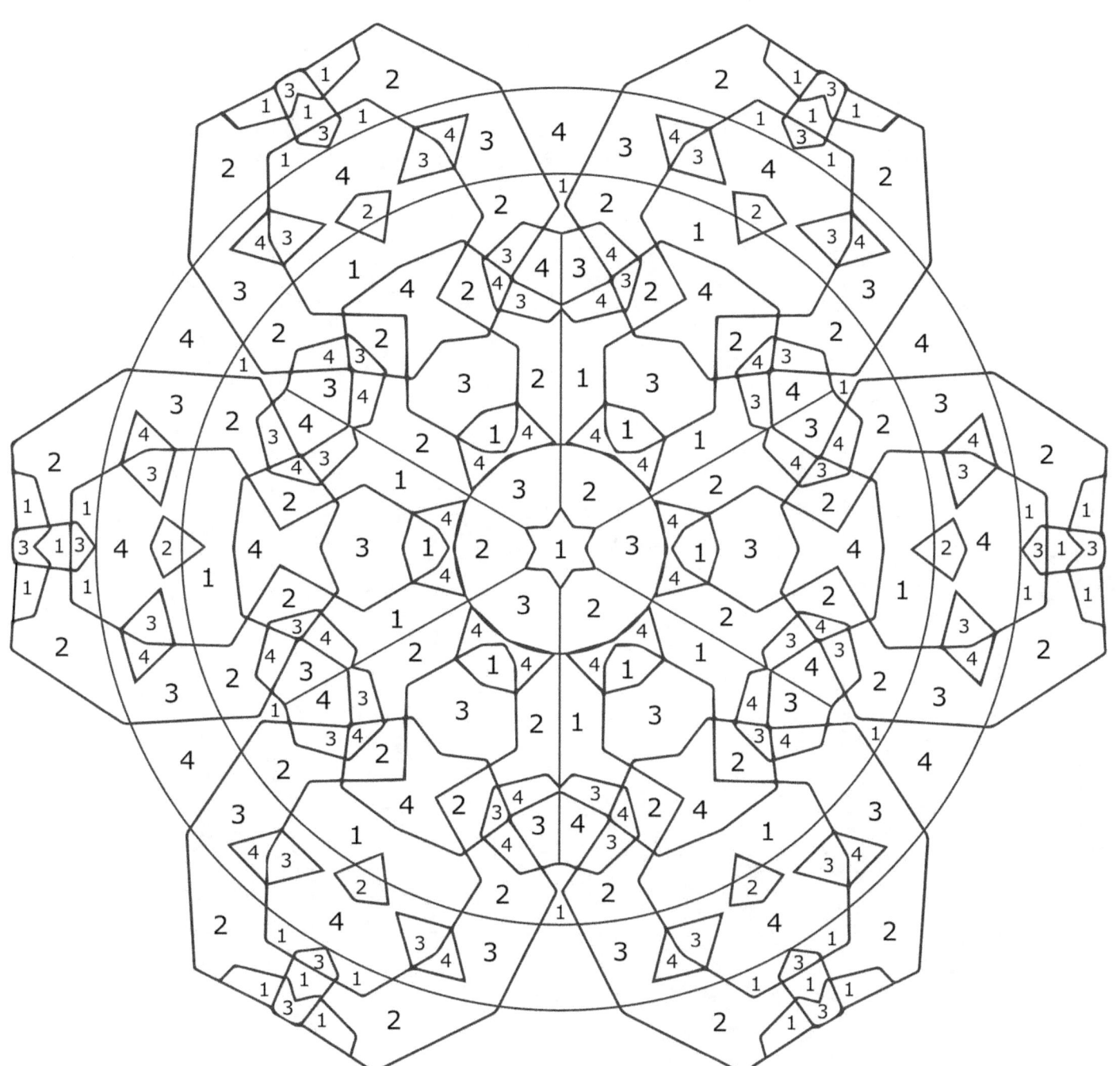

Suggested Colors:

1. Canary Yellow

2. Yellowed Orange

3. Aquamarine

4. Parma Violet

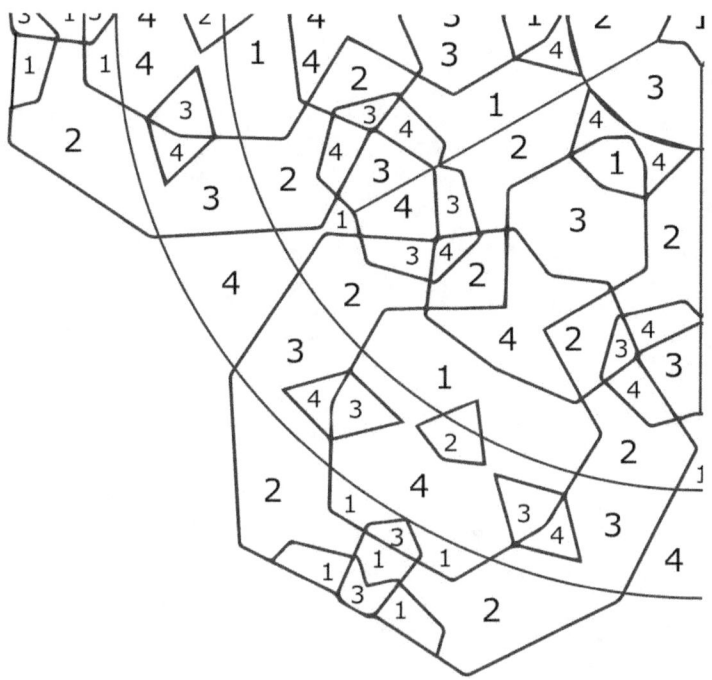

Test New Colors:

1.

2.

3.

4.

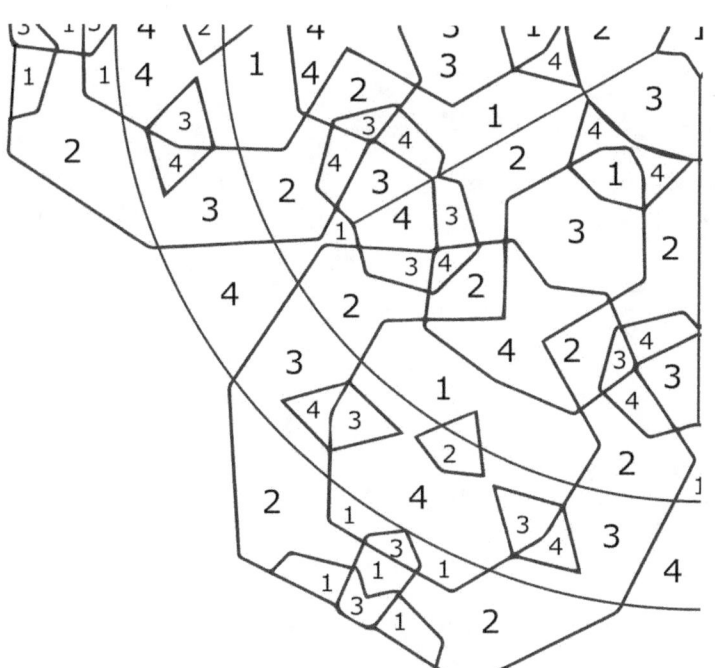

Test New Colors:

1.

2.

3.

4.

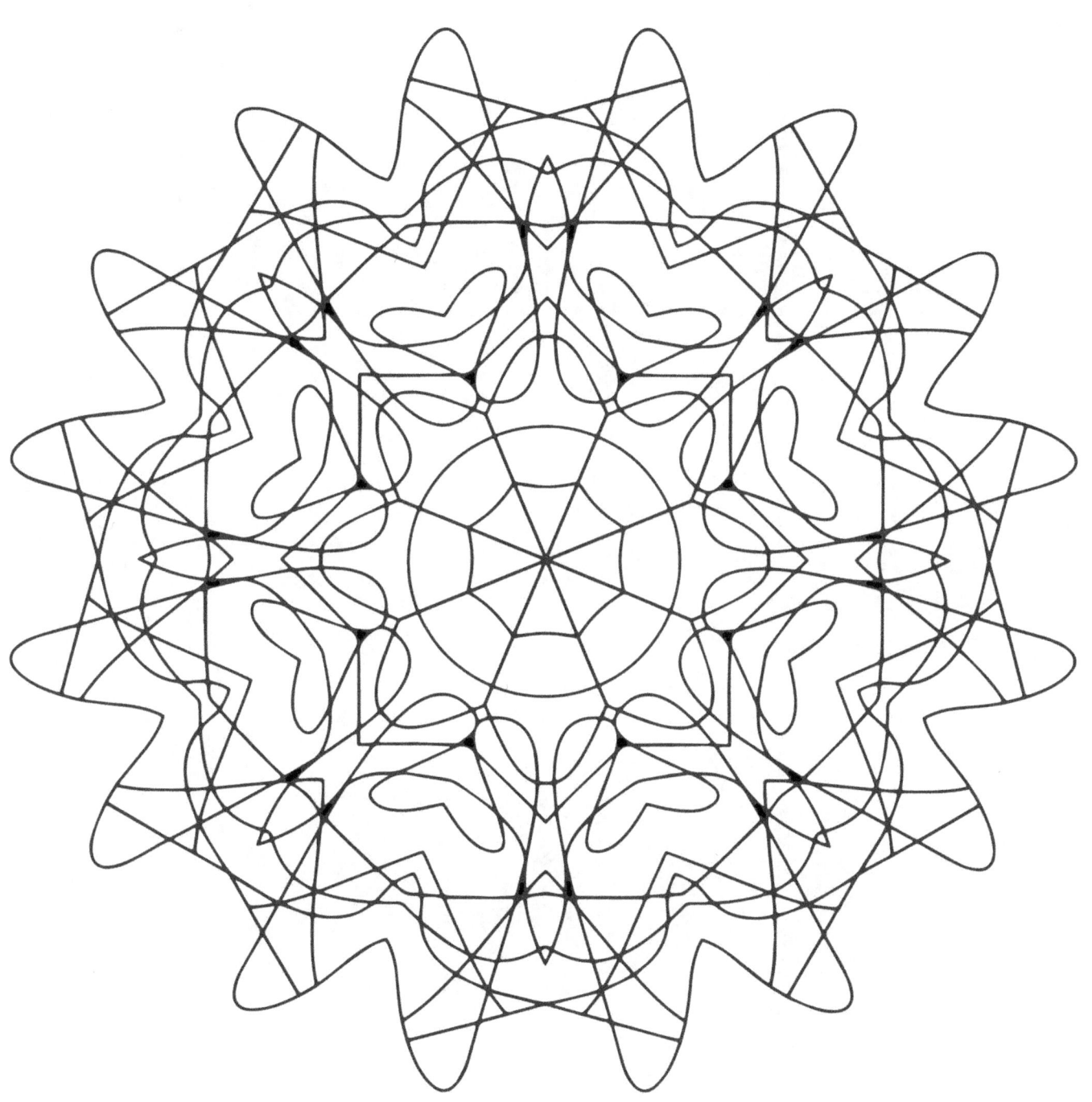

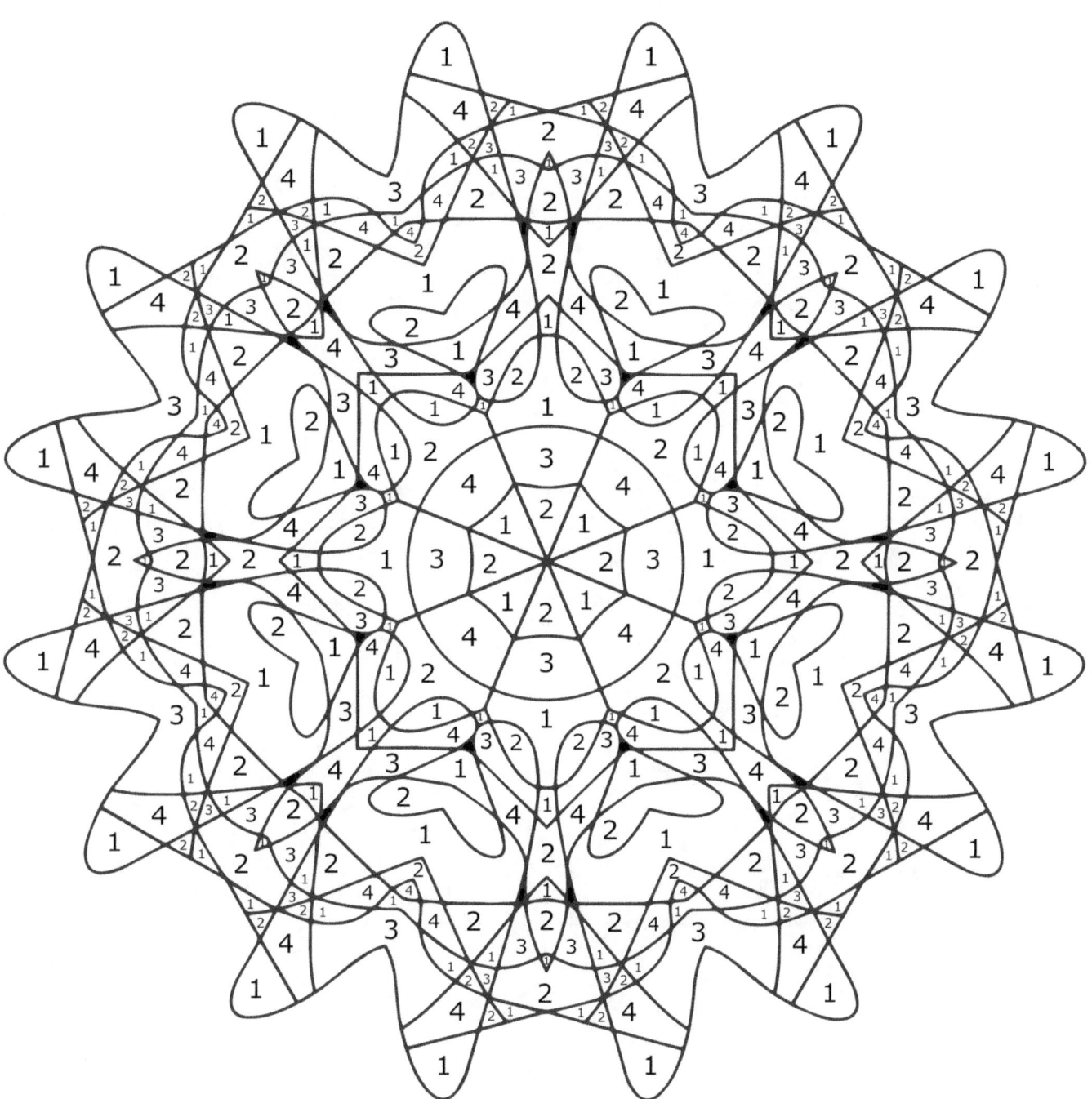

Suggested Colors:

1. Light Aqua

4. Indigo Blue

2. Process Red

3. Parma Violet

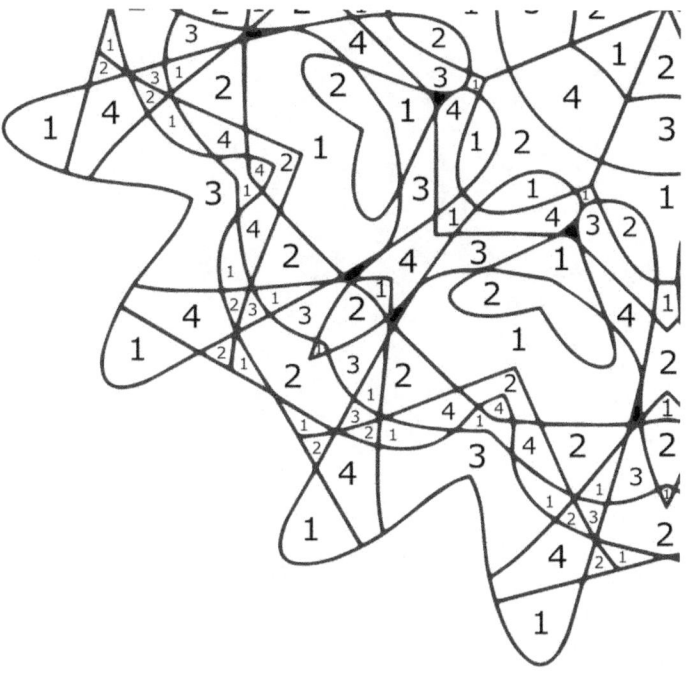

Test New Colors:

1.

2.

3.

4.

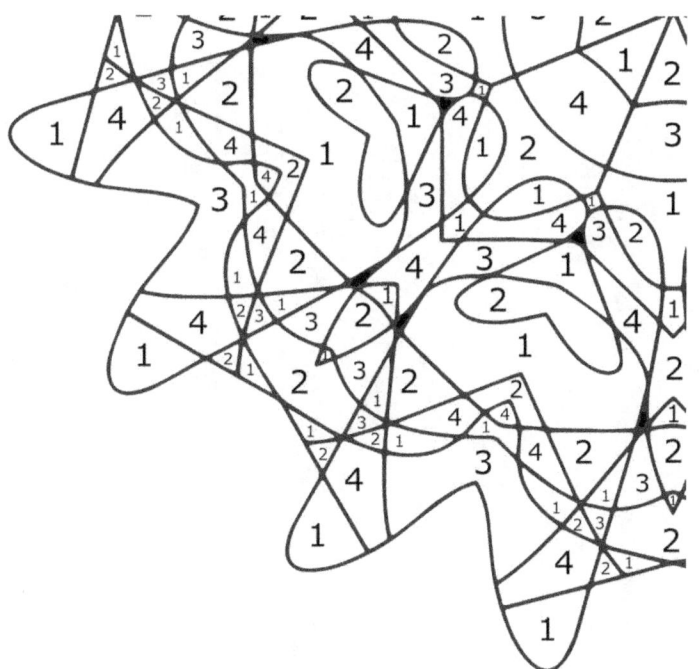

Test New Colors:

1.

2.

3.

4.

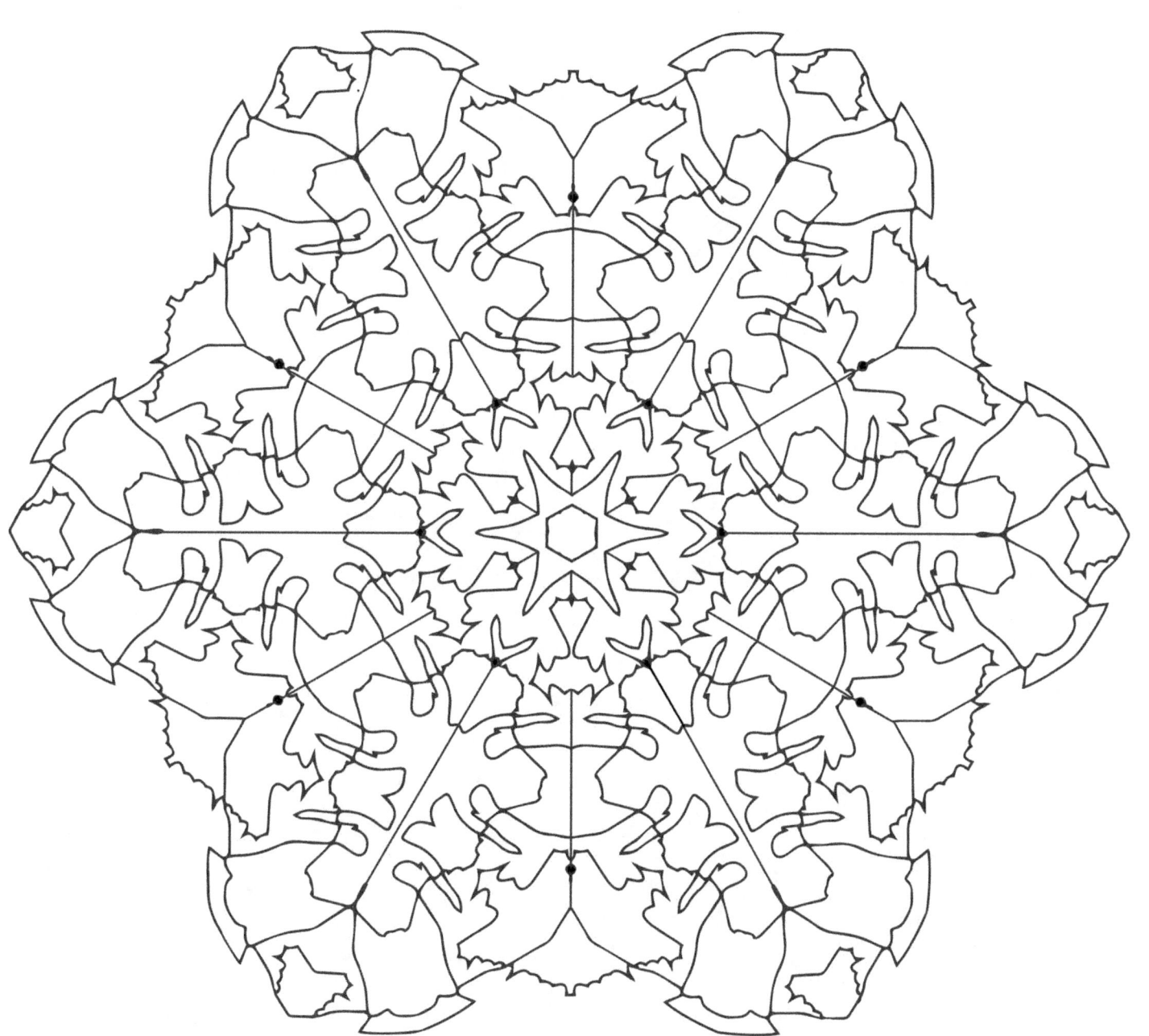

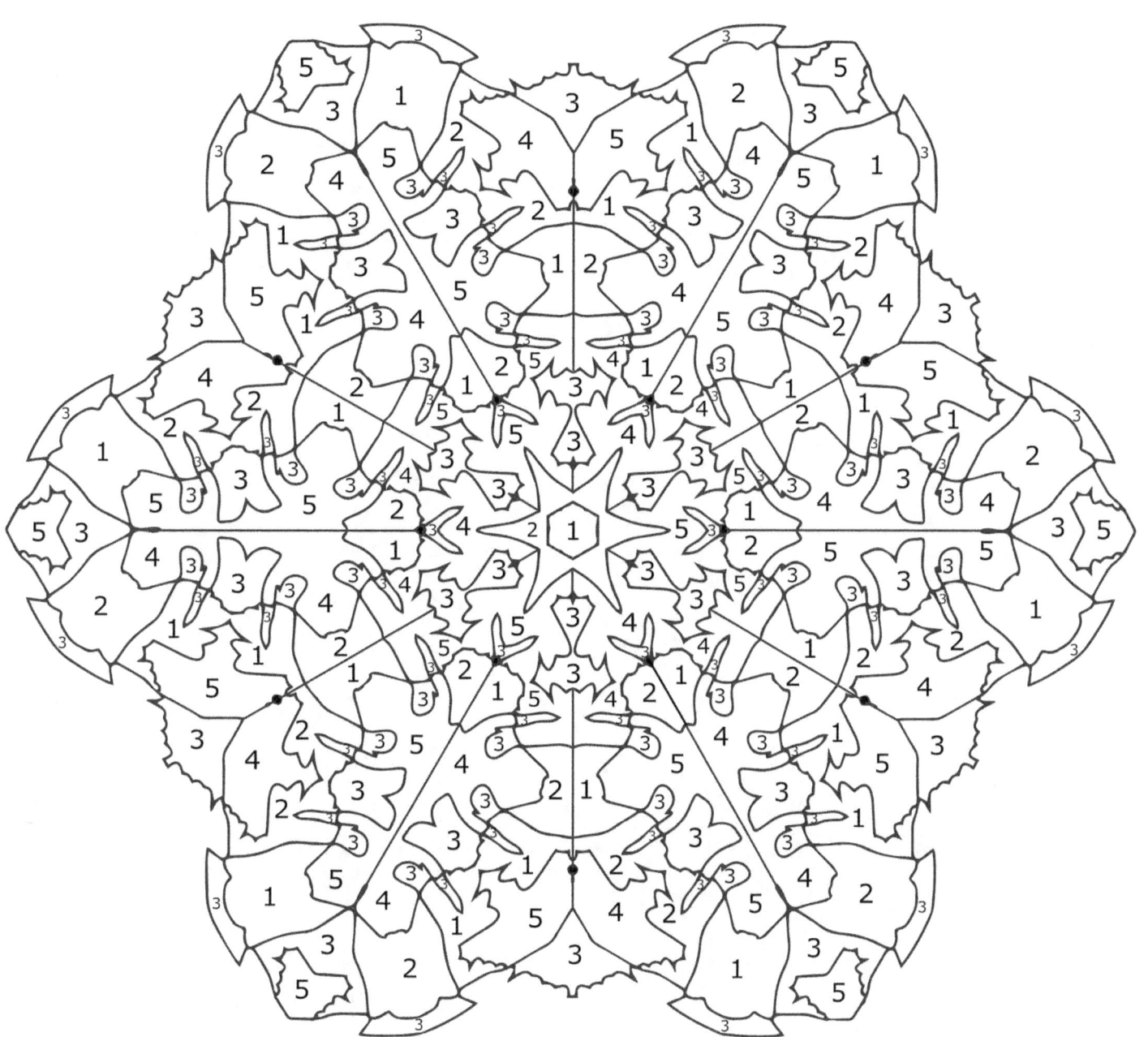

Suggested Colors:

1. Canary Yellow

2. Spring Green

3. Process Red

4. Parma Violet

5. Light Cerulean Blue

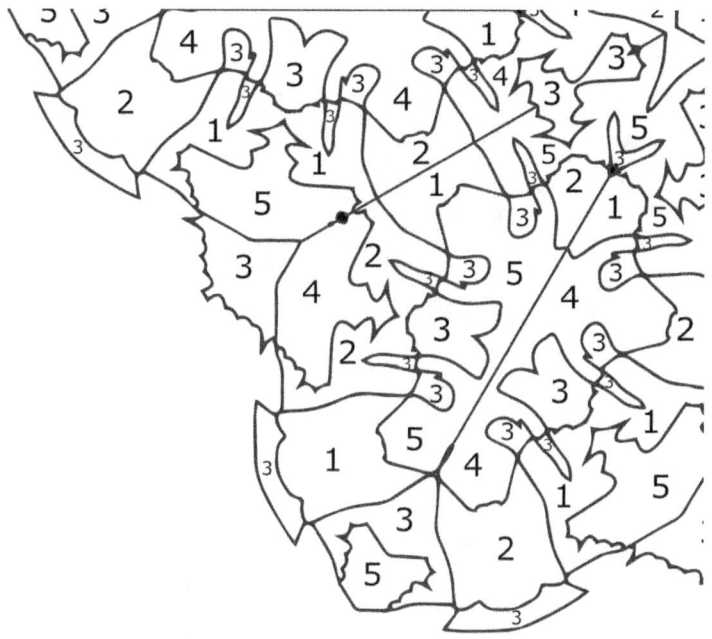

Test New Colors:

1.

2.

3.

4.

5.

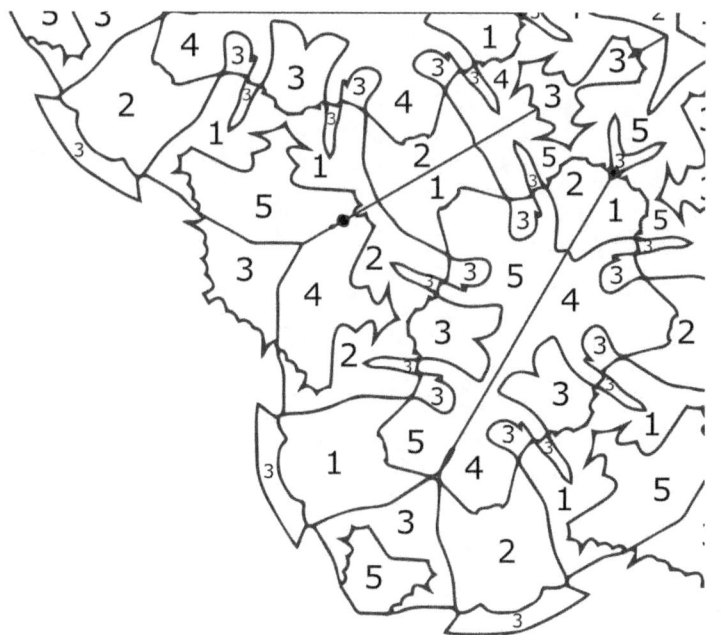

Test New Colors:

1.

2.

3.

4.

5.

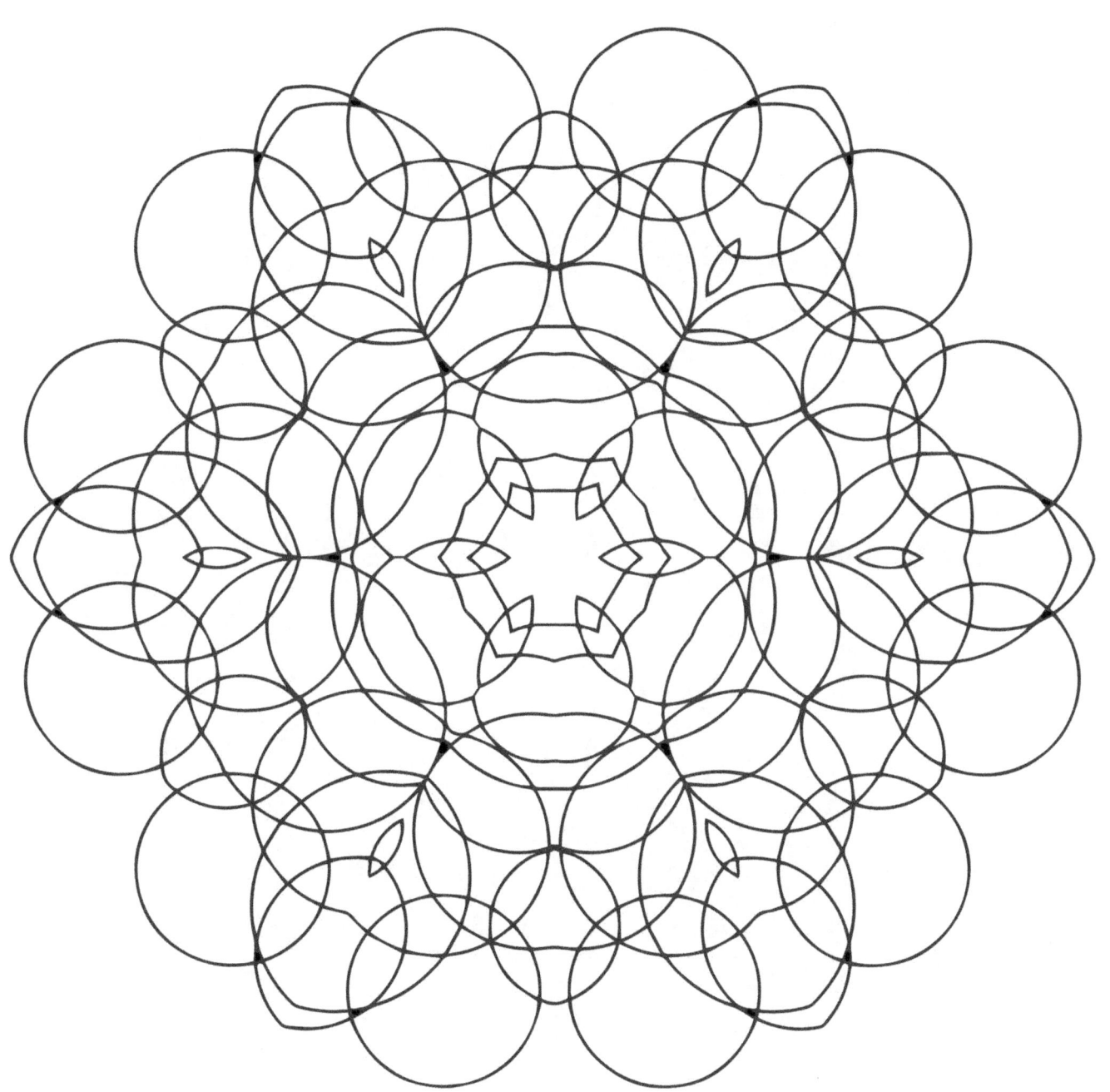

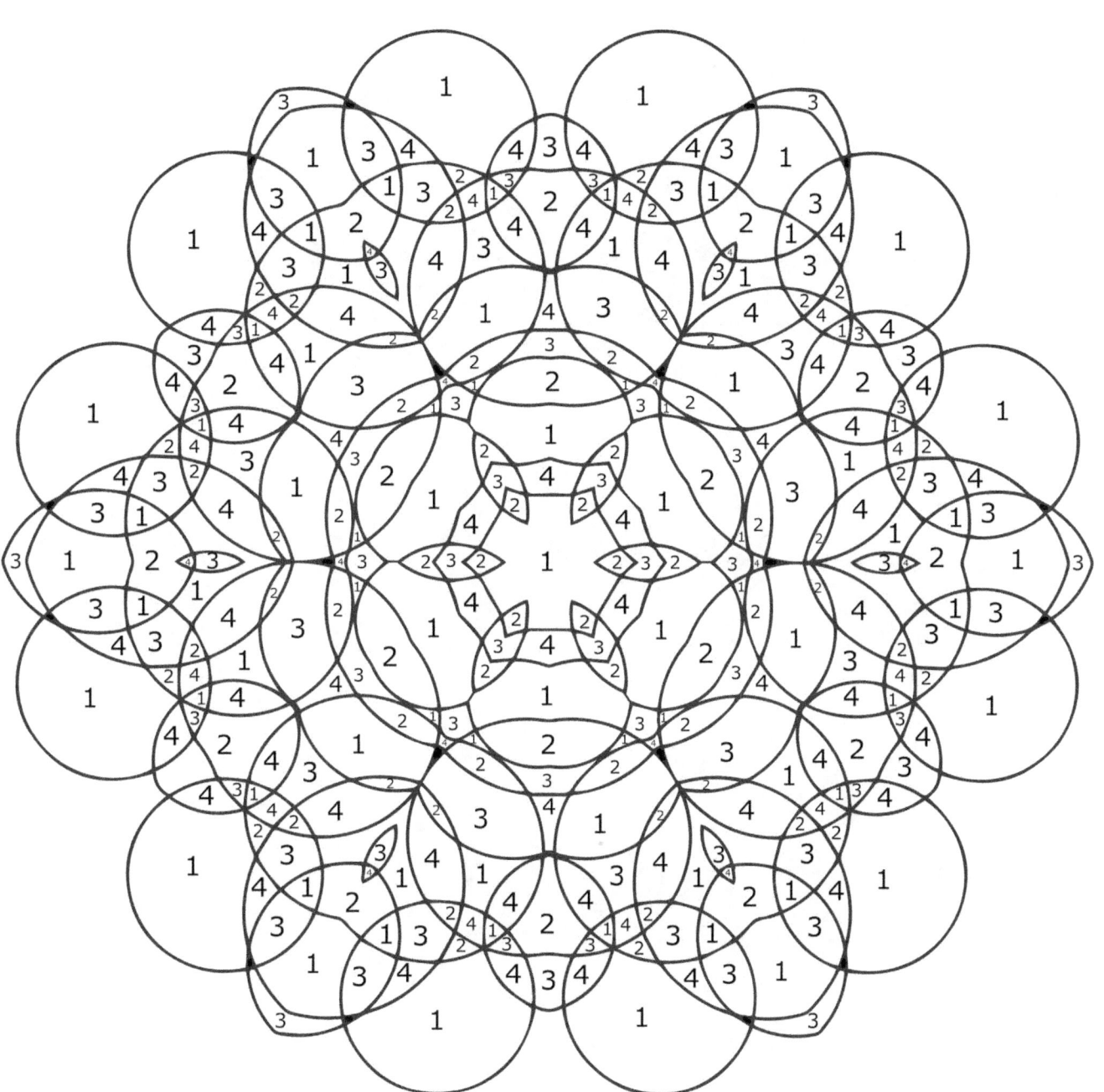

Suggested Colors:

1. Canary Yellow   4. Violet Blue

2. Spring Green

3. Aquamarine

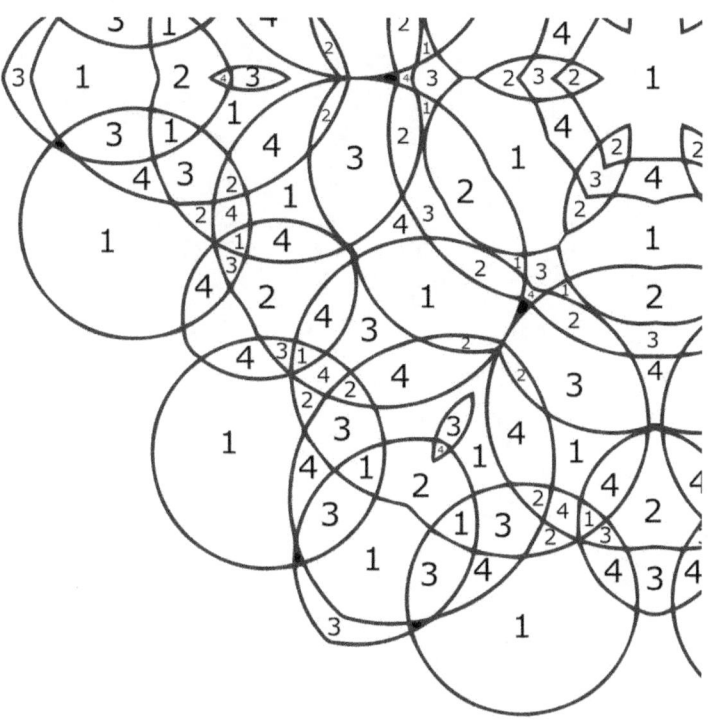

Test New Colors:

1.

2.

3.

4.

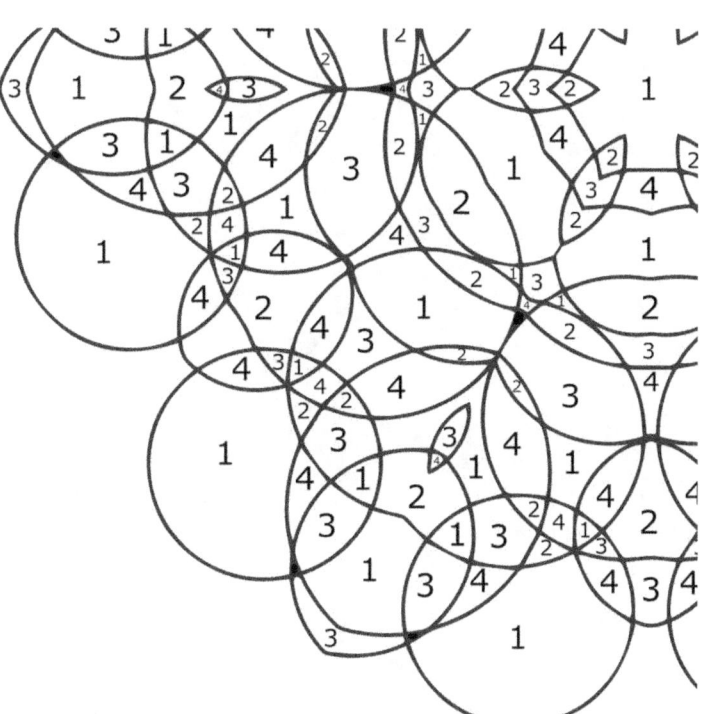

Test New Colors:

1.

2.

3.

4.

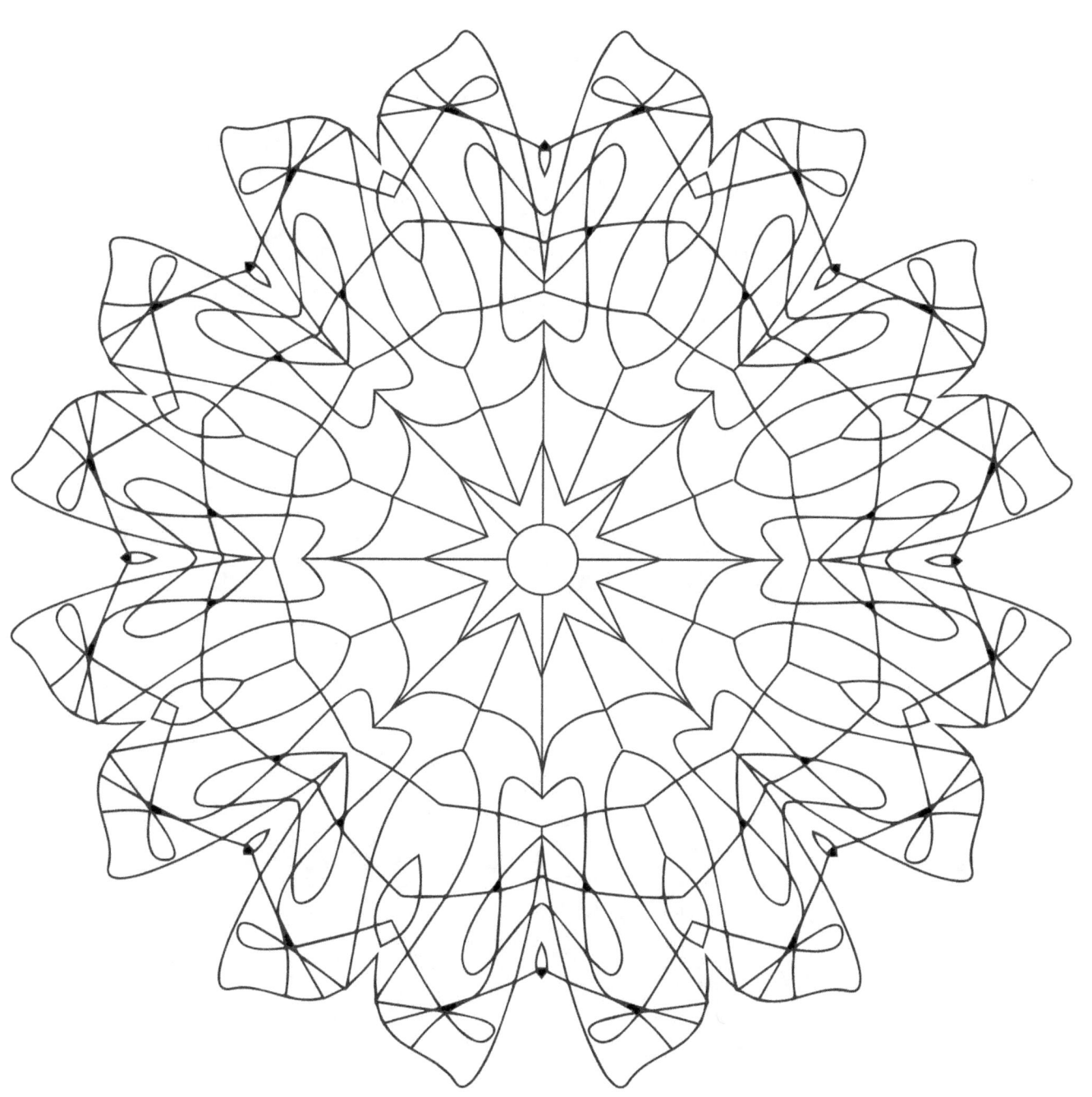

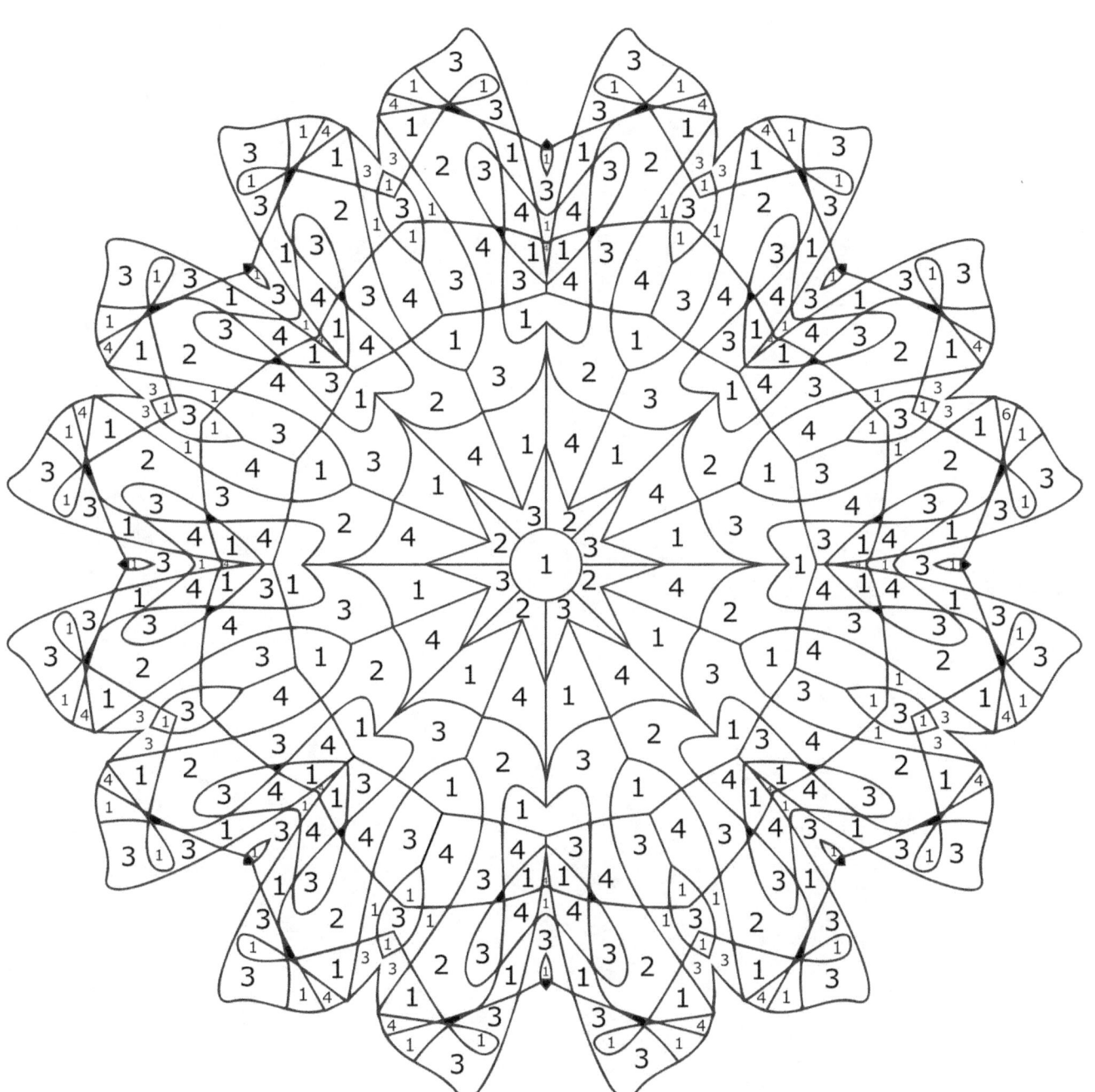

Suggested Colors:

1. Spring Green   4. Dark Green

2. Apple Green

3. Grass Green

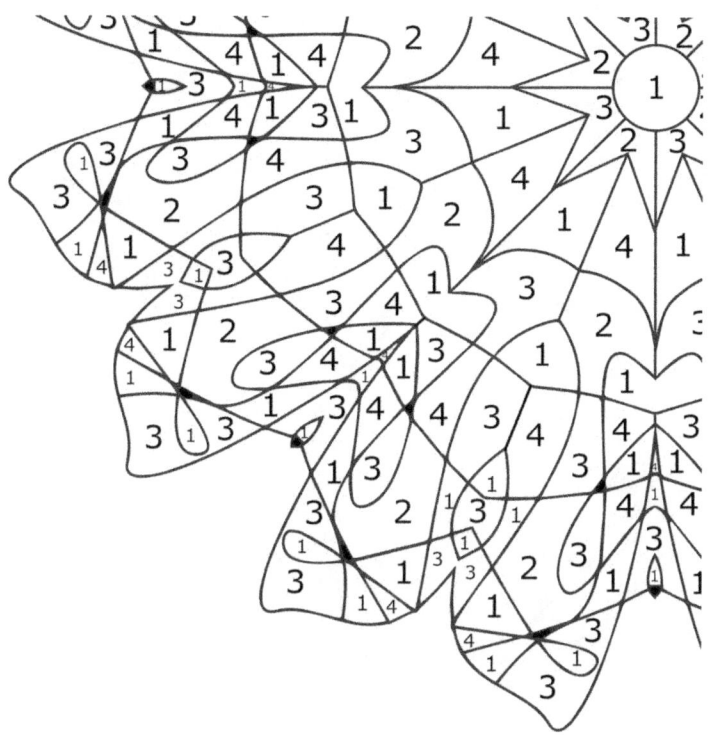

Test New Colors:

1.

2.

3.

4.

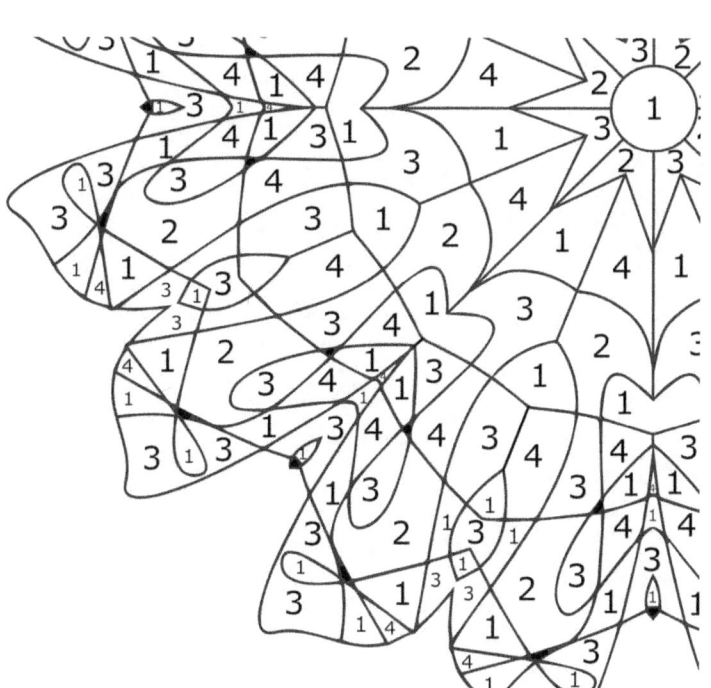

Test New Colors:

1.

2.

3.

4.

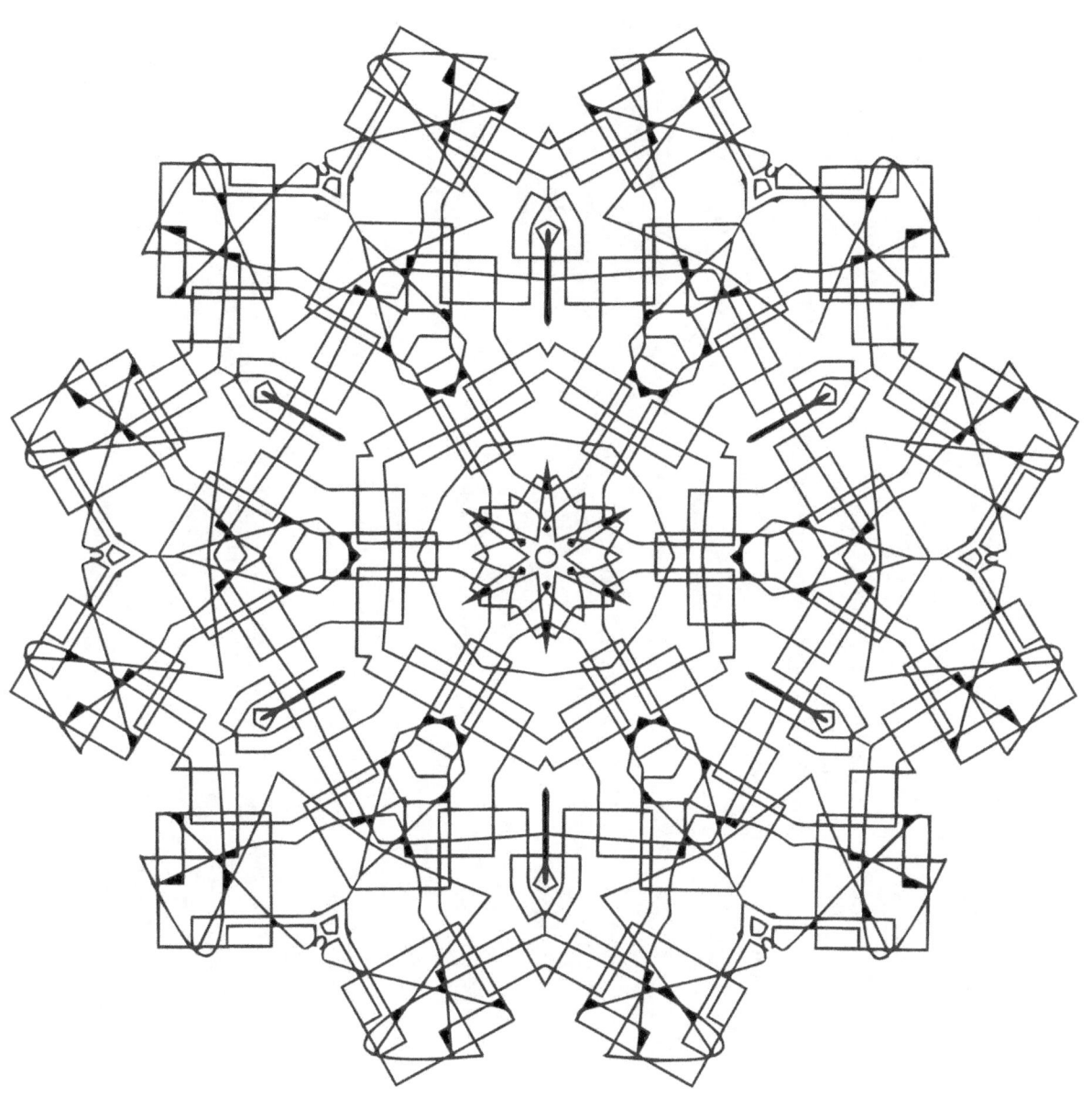

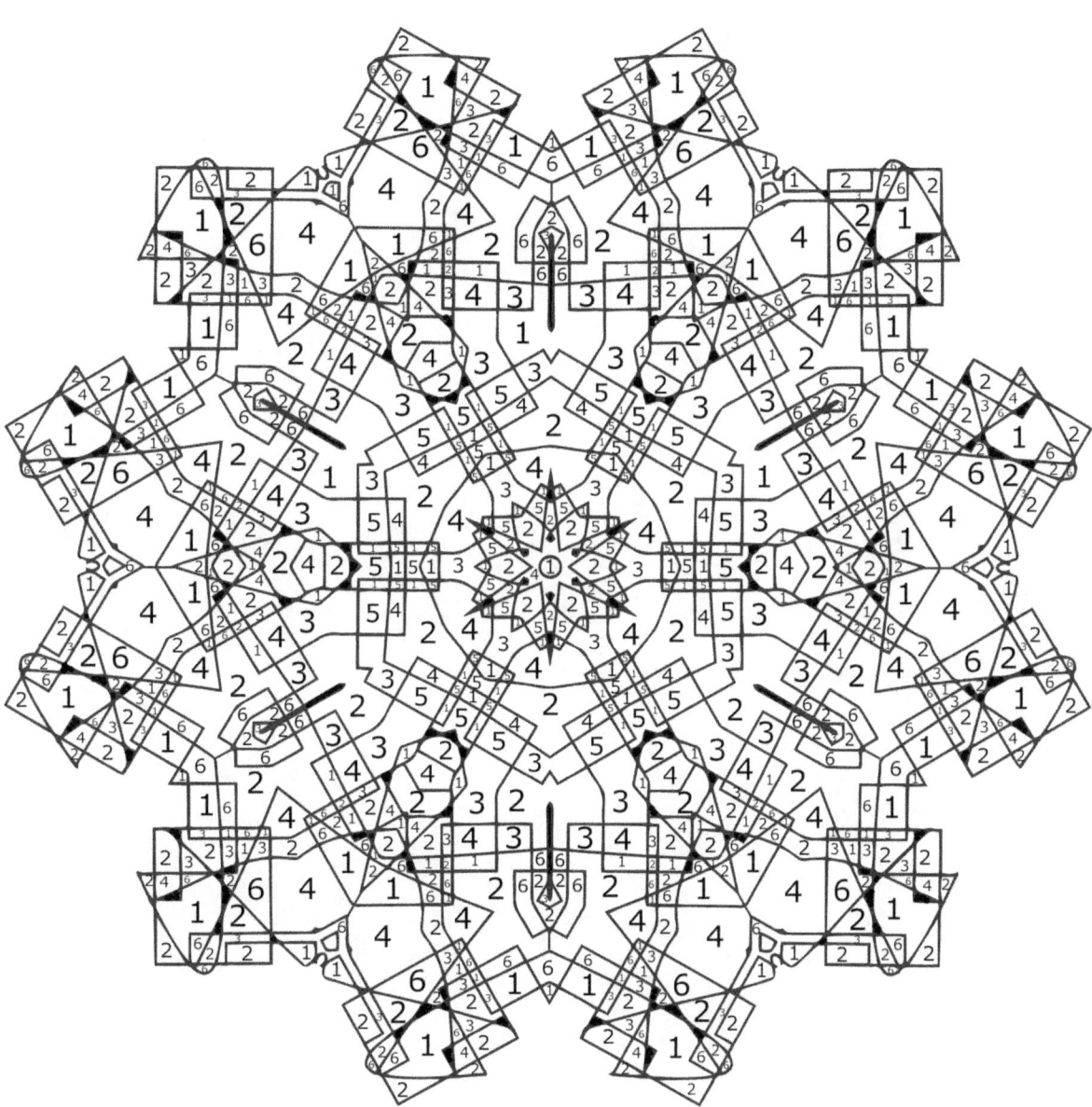

Suggested Colors:

1. Aquamarine   4. True Blue

2. Electric Blue   5. Indigo Blue

3. Peacock Blue   6. Violet Blue

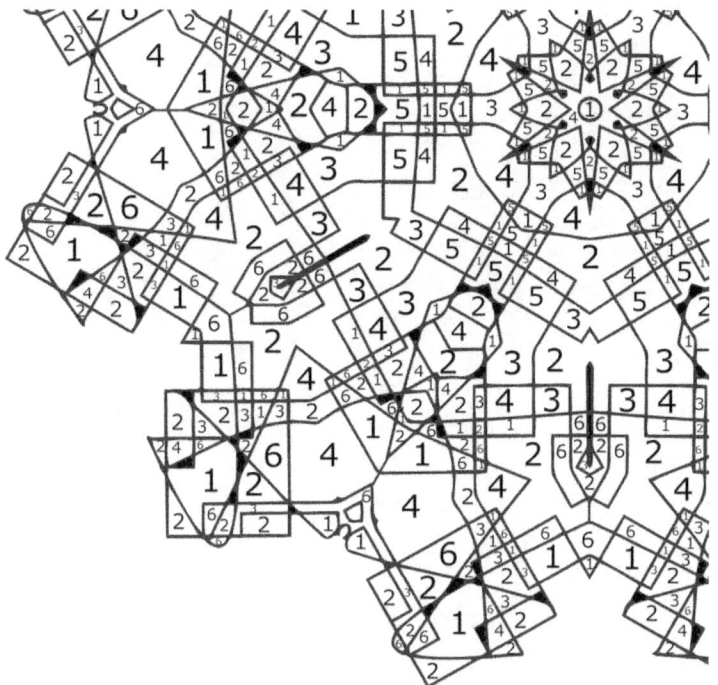

Test New Colors:

1.

2.

3.

4.

5.

6.

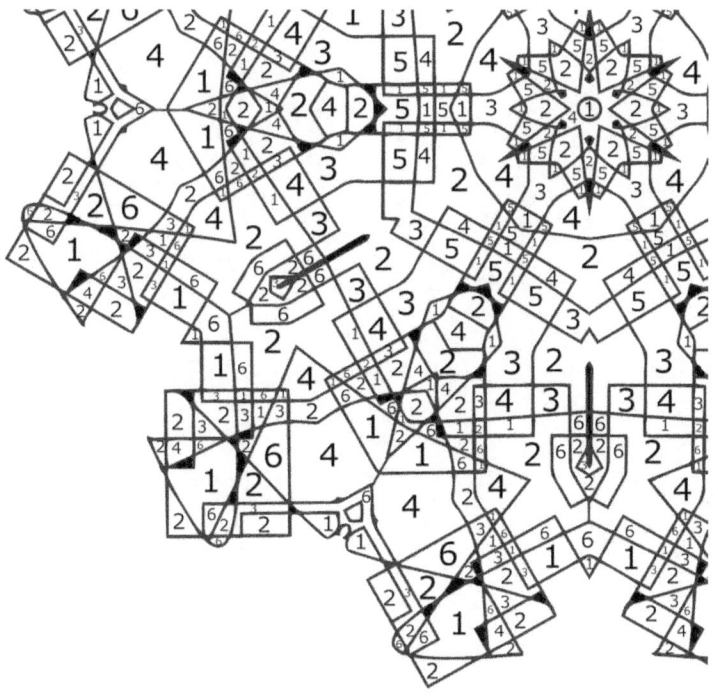

Test New Colors:

1.

2.

3.

4.

5.

6.

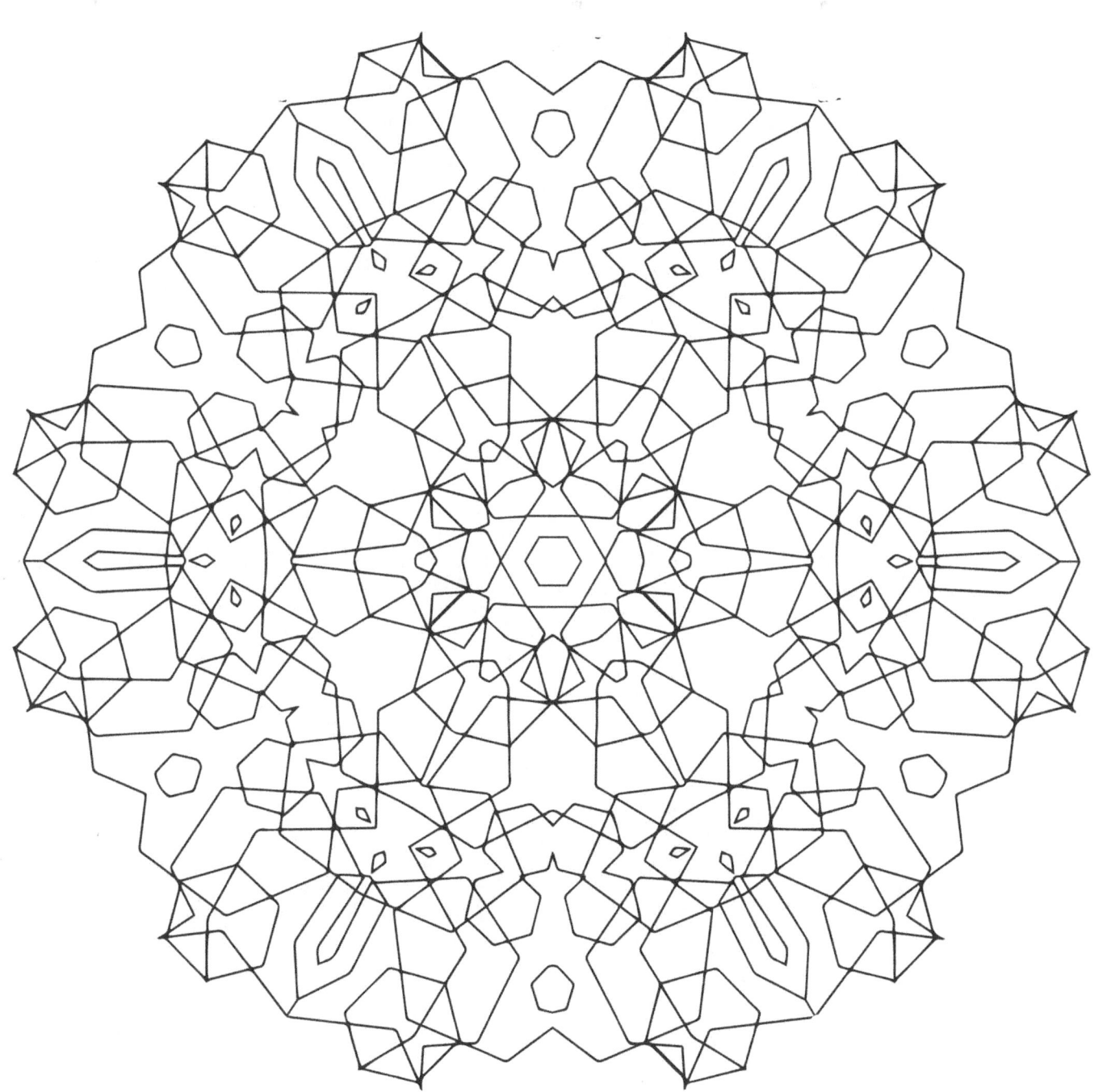

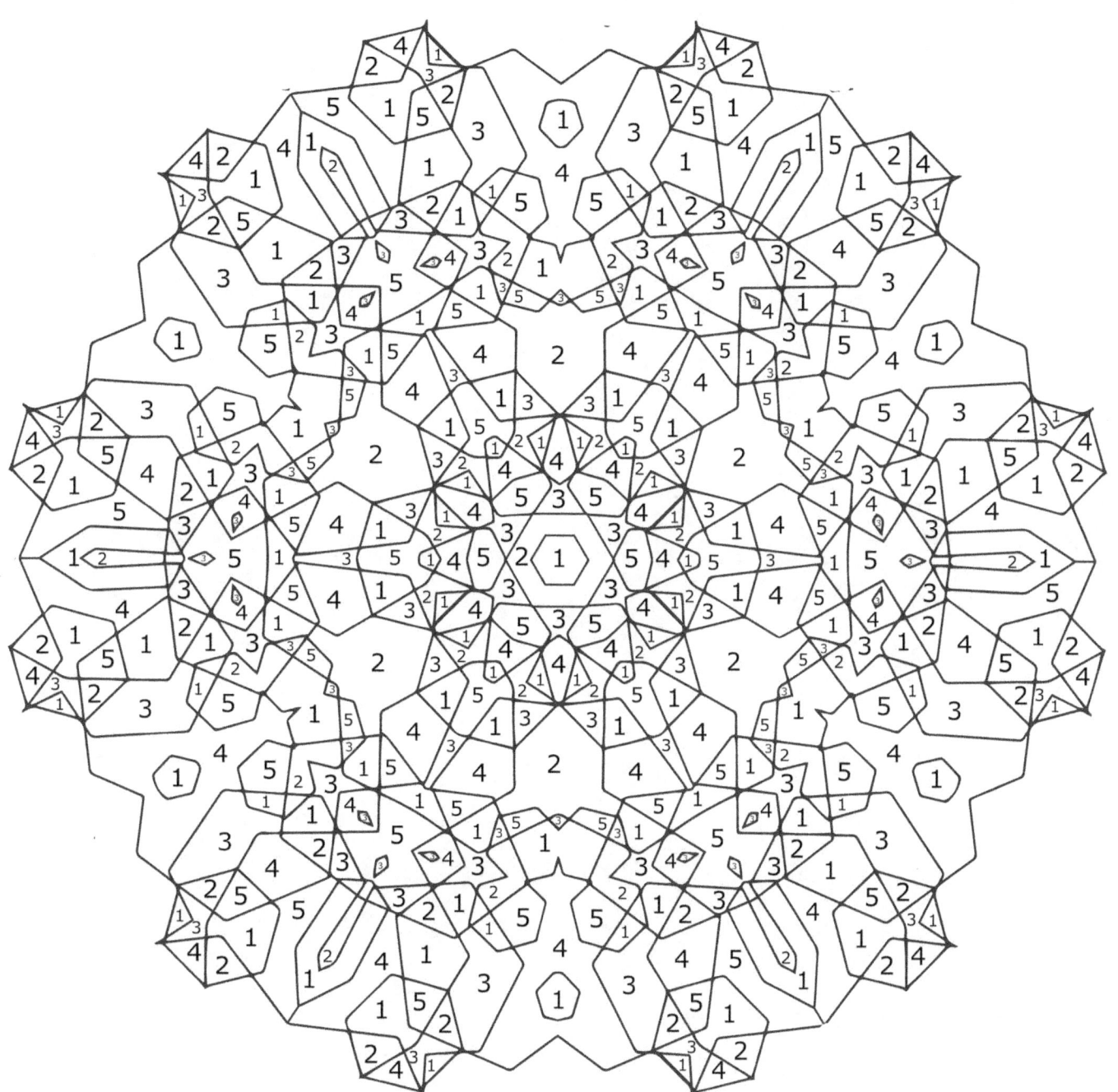

Suggested Colors:

1. Canary Yellow
4. Parma Violet

2. Spring Green
5. Light Cerulean Blue

3. Process Red

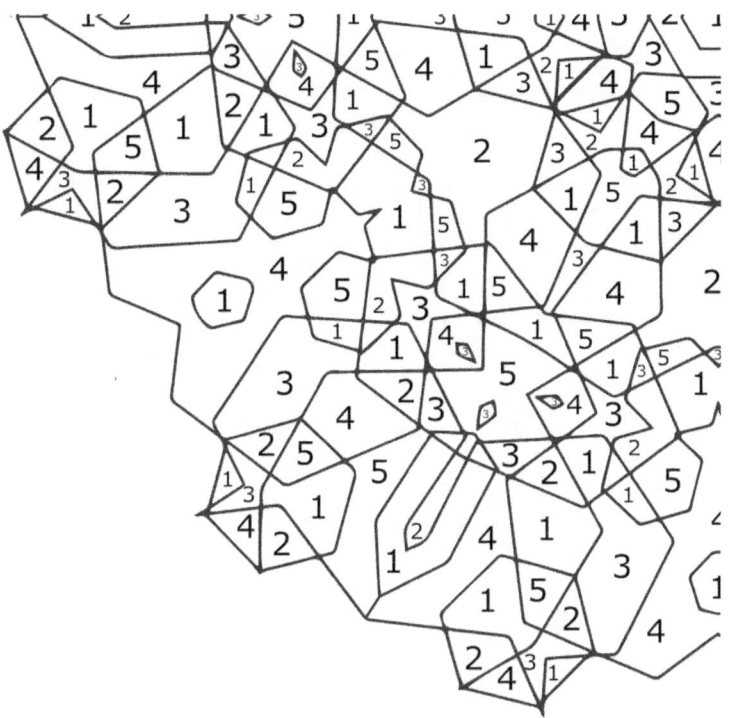

Test New Colors:

1.

2.

3.

4.

5.

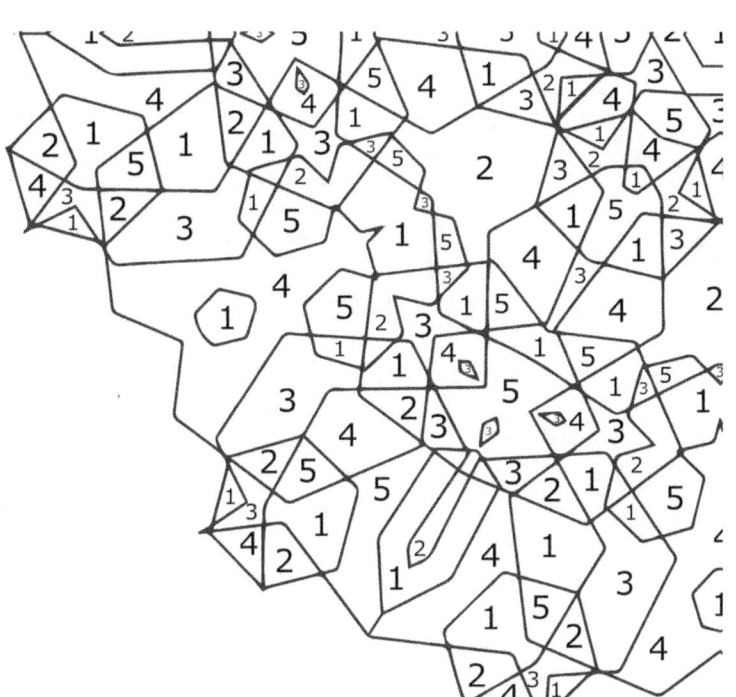

Test New Colors:

1.

2.

3.

4.

5.

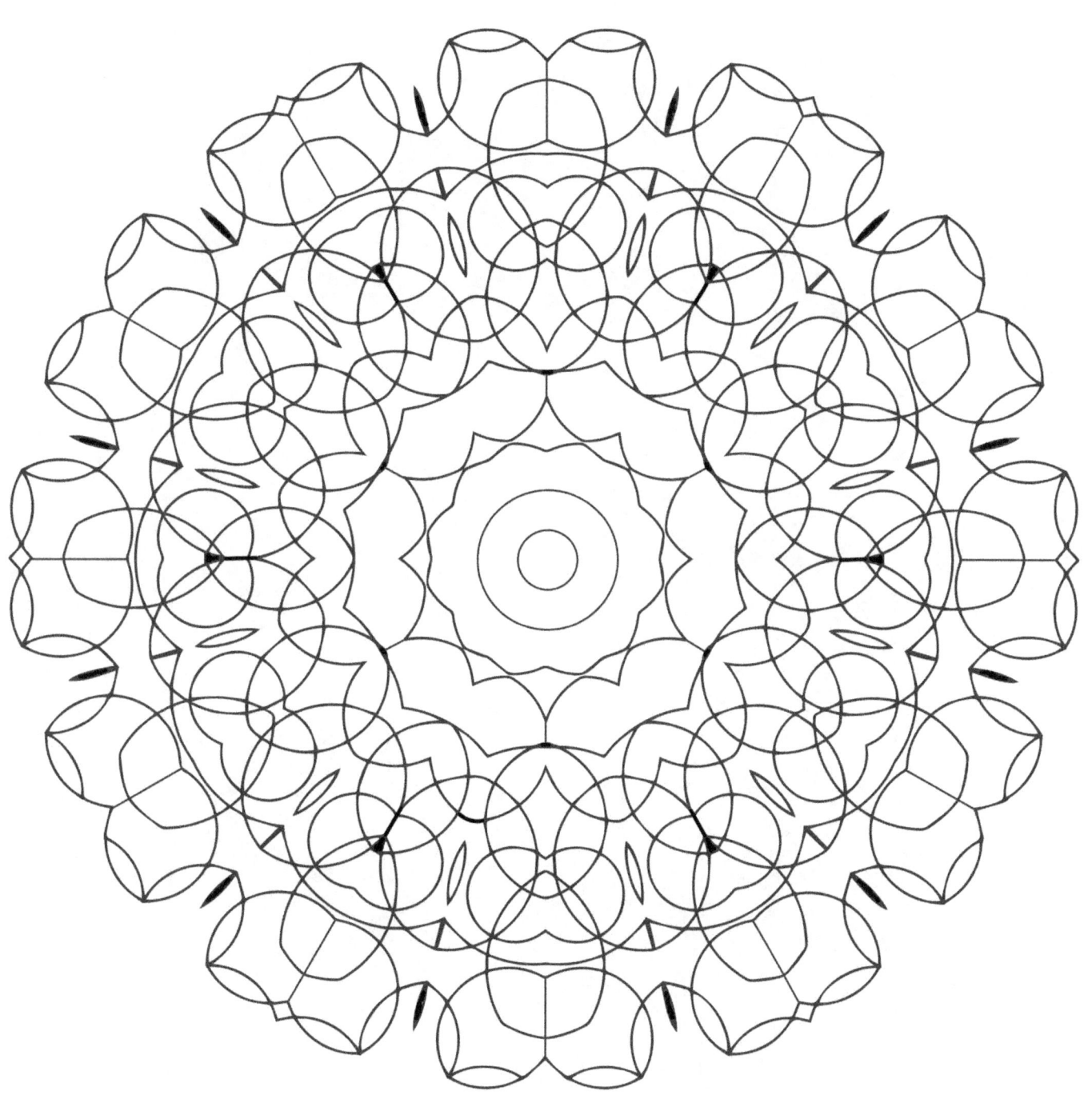

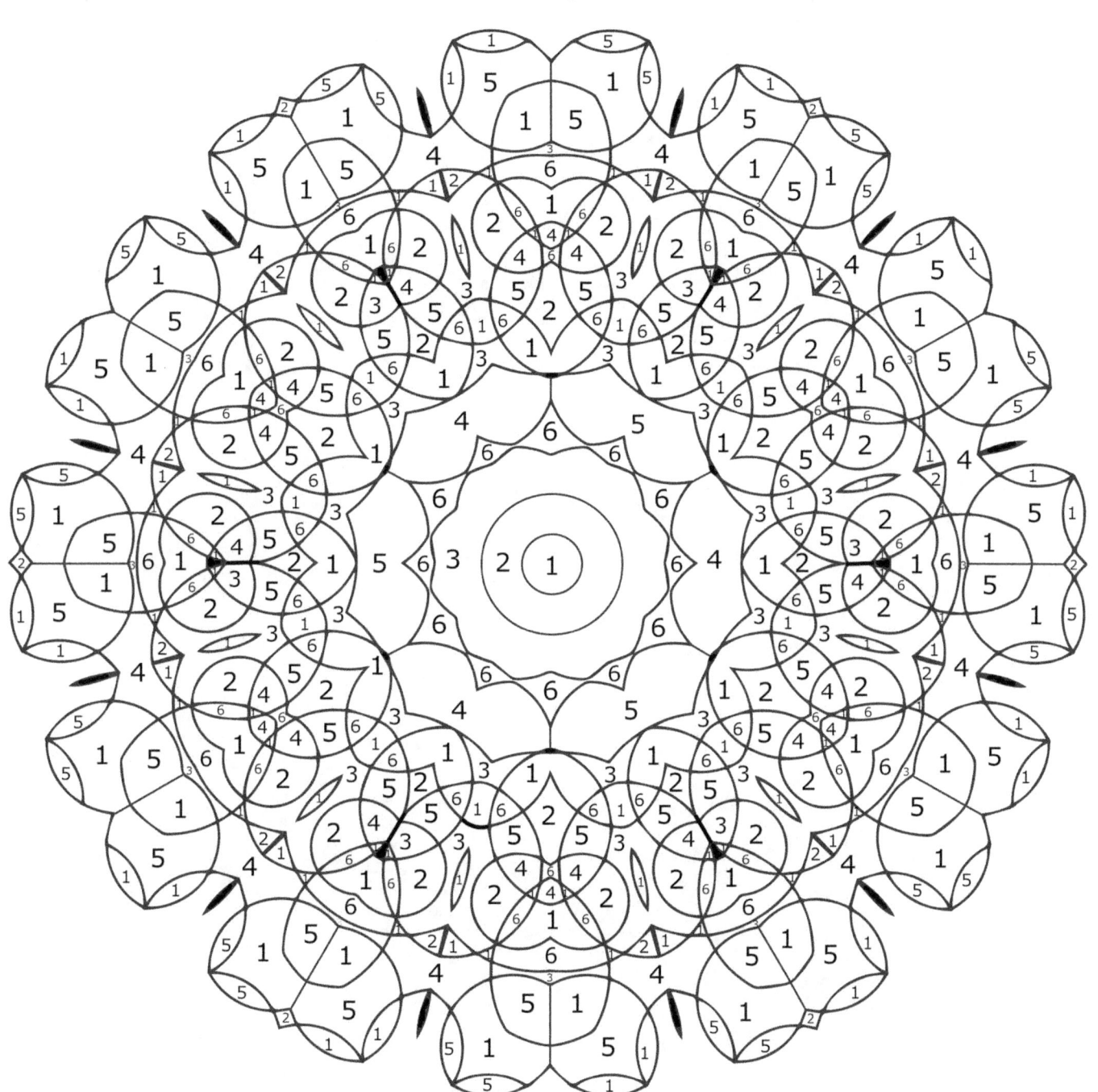

Suggested Colors:

1. Sunburst Yellow

2. Apple Green

3. Scarlet Lake

4. Magenta

5. Dahlia Purple

6. Electric Blue

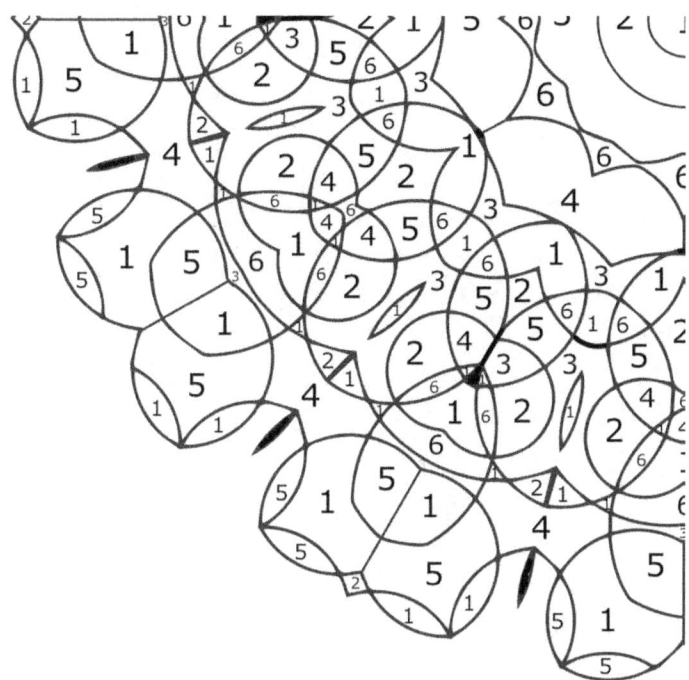

Test New Colors:

1.

2.

3.

4.

5.

6.

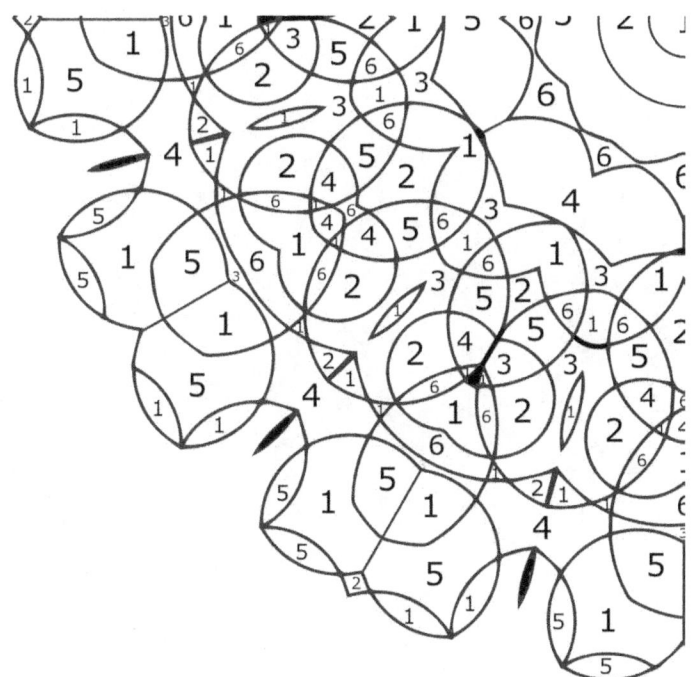

Test New Colors:

1.

2.

3.

4.

5.

6.

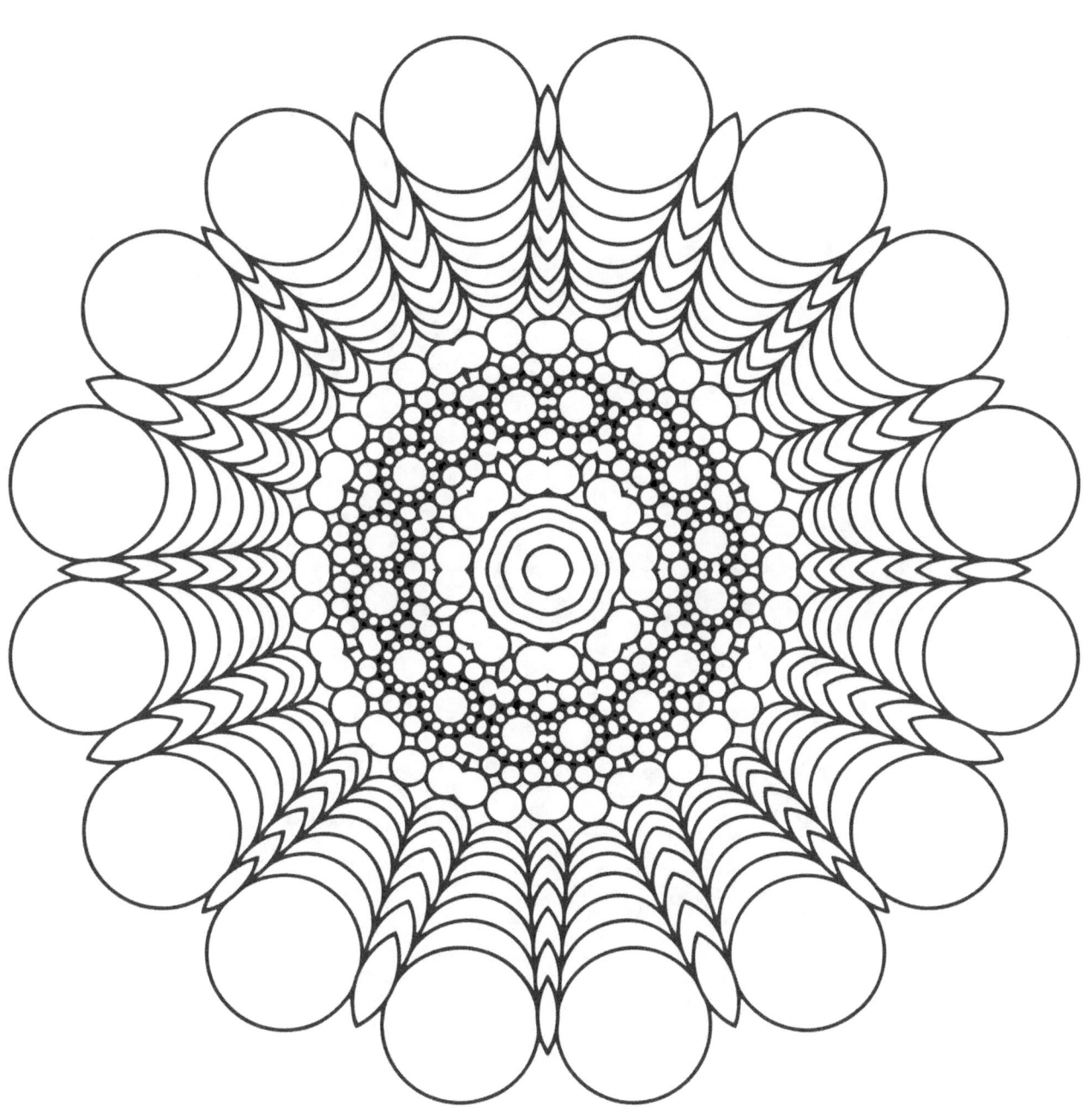

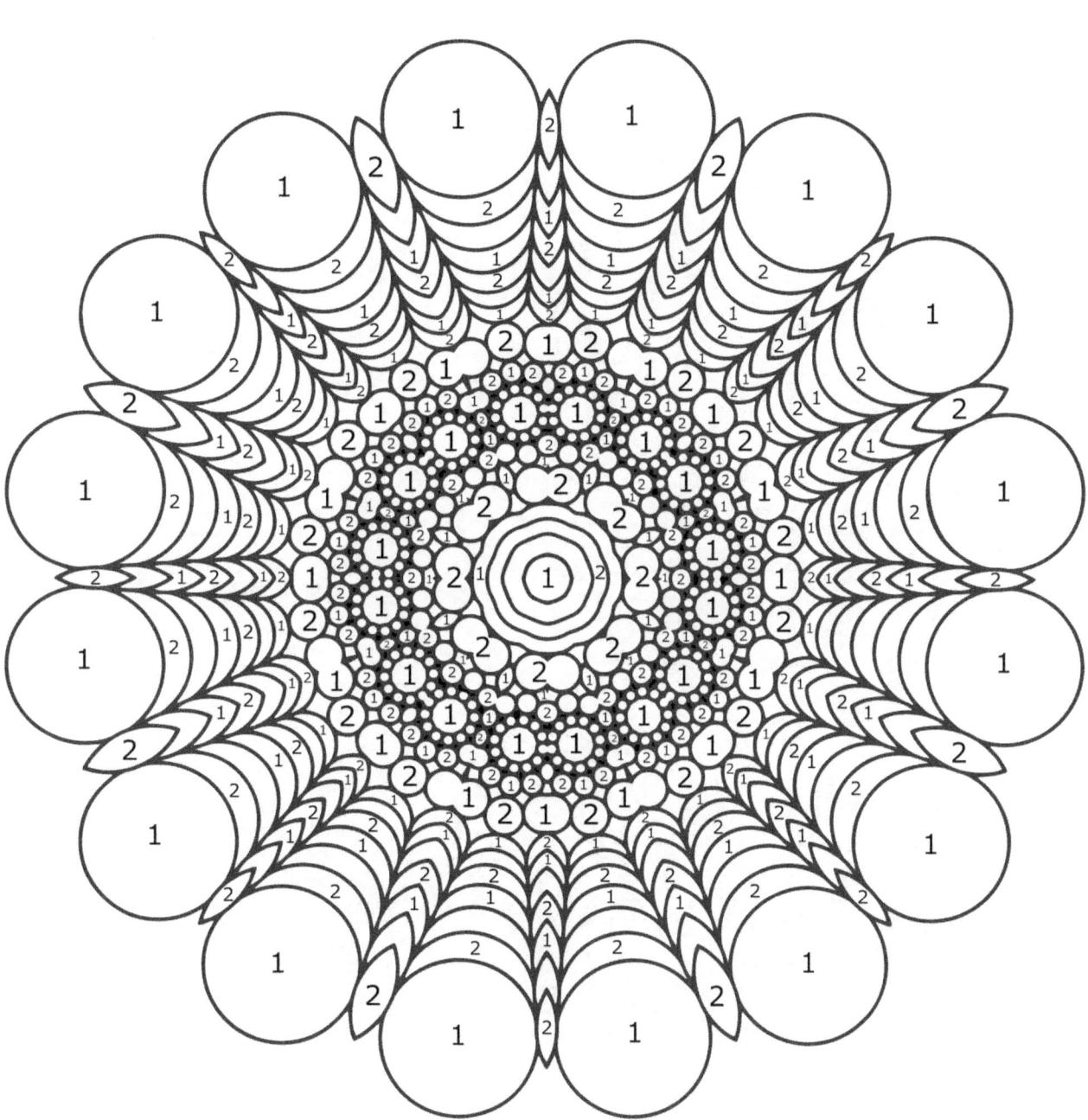

Suggested Colors:

1. Scarlet Red

2. Violet Blue

3. WHITE (not numbered)

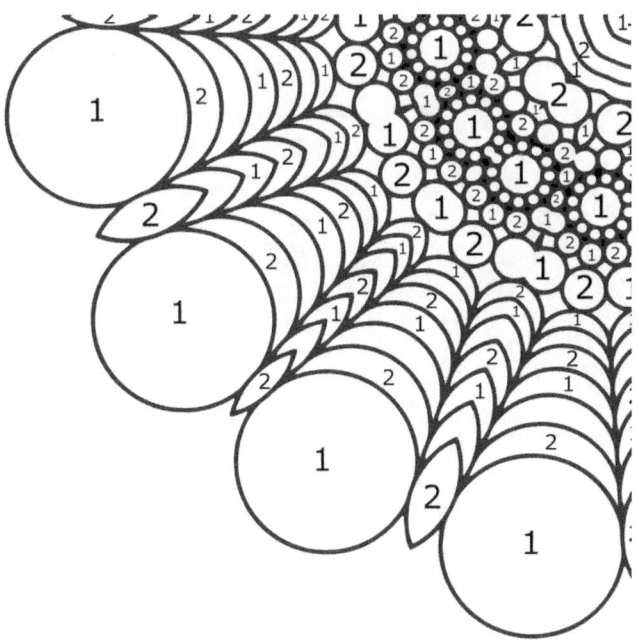

Test New Colors:

1.

2.

3. (not numbered)

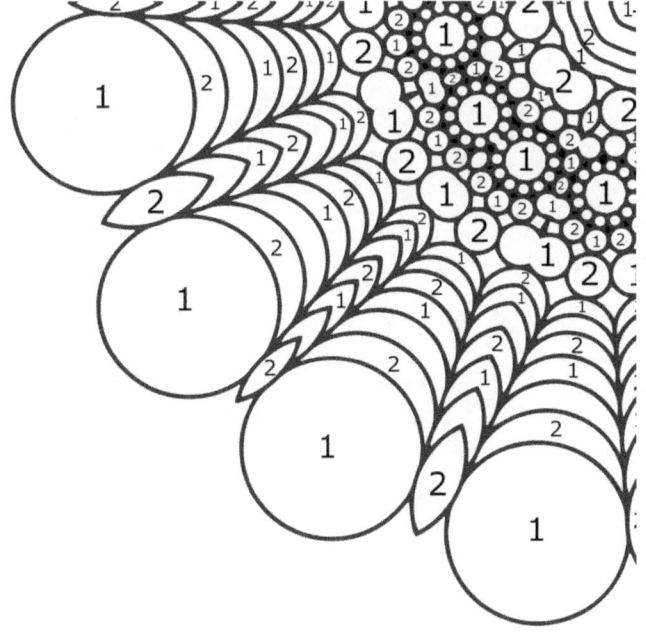

Test New Colors:

1.

2.

3. (not numbered

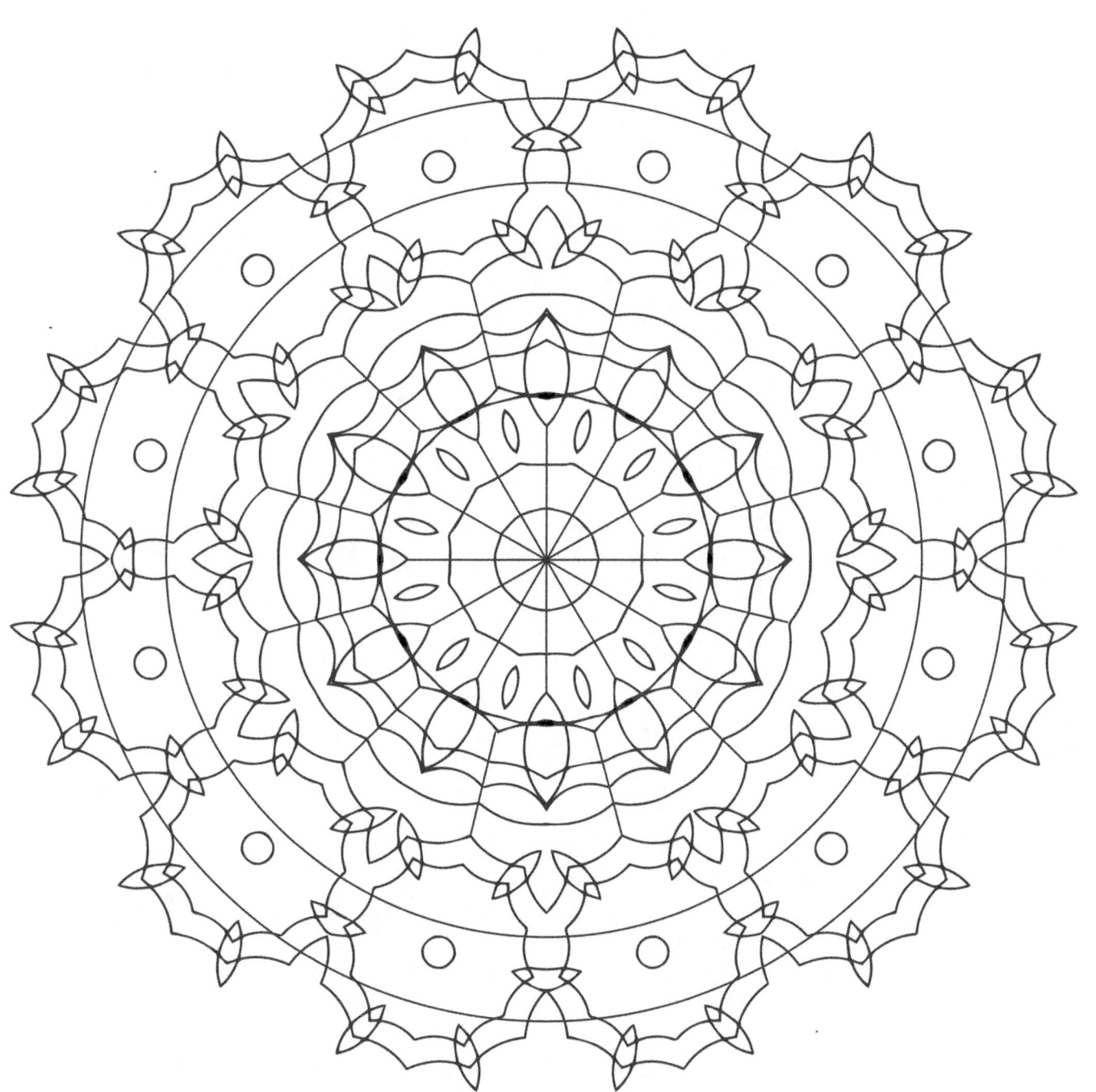

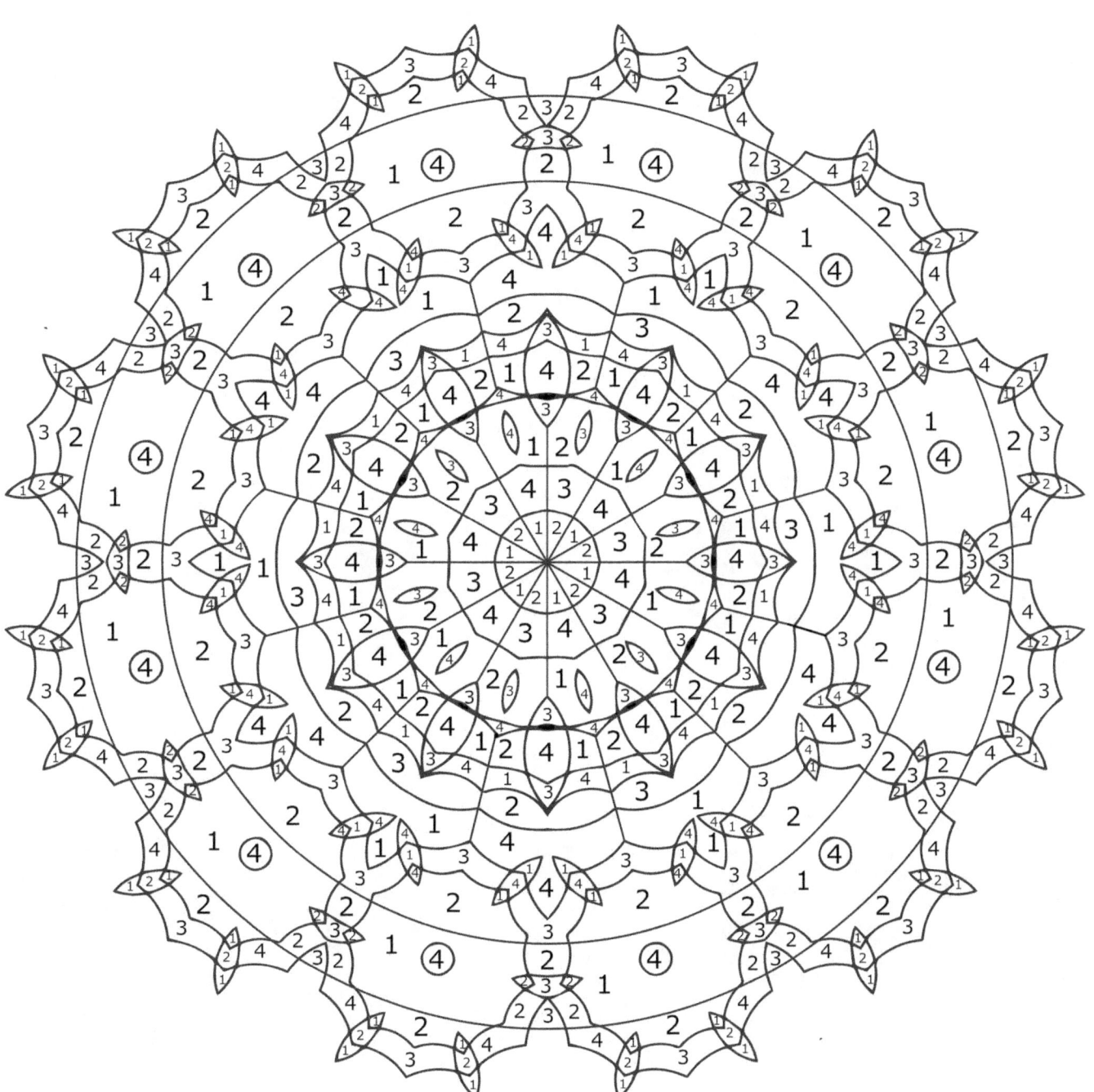

Suggested Colors:

1. Canary Yellow

2. Yellowed Orange

3. Aquamarine

4. Parma Violet

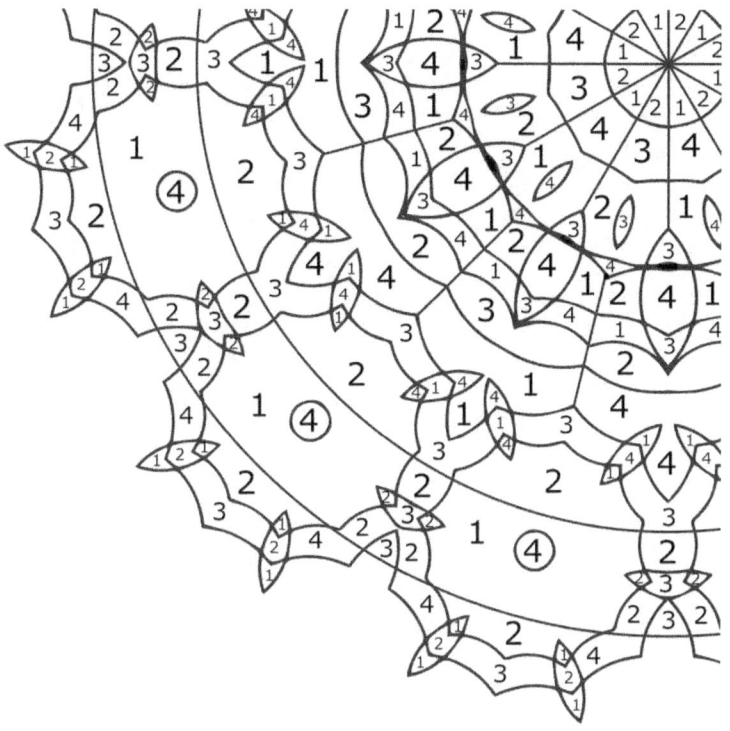

Test New Colors:

1.

2.

3.

4.

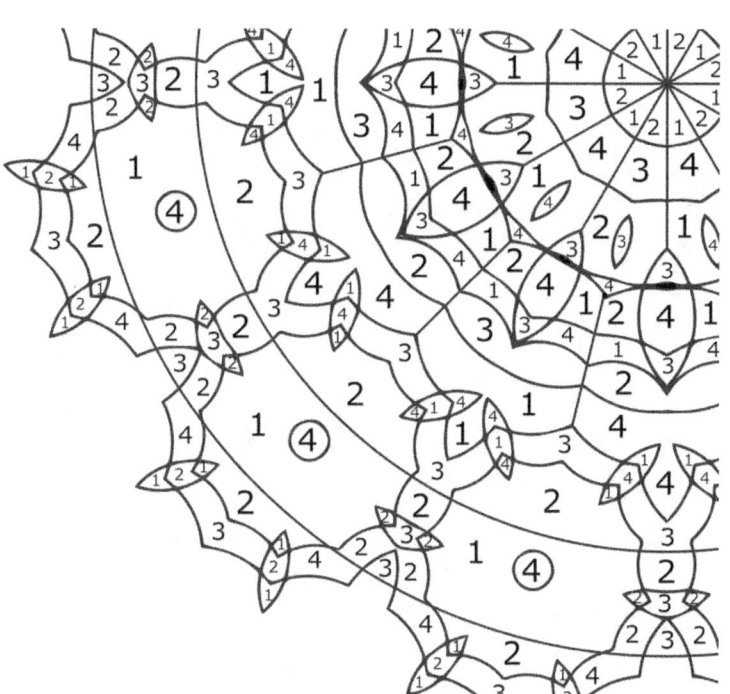

Test New Colors:

1.

2.

3.

4.

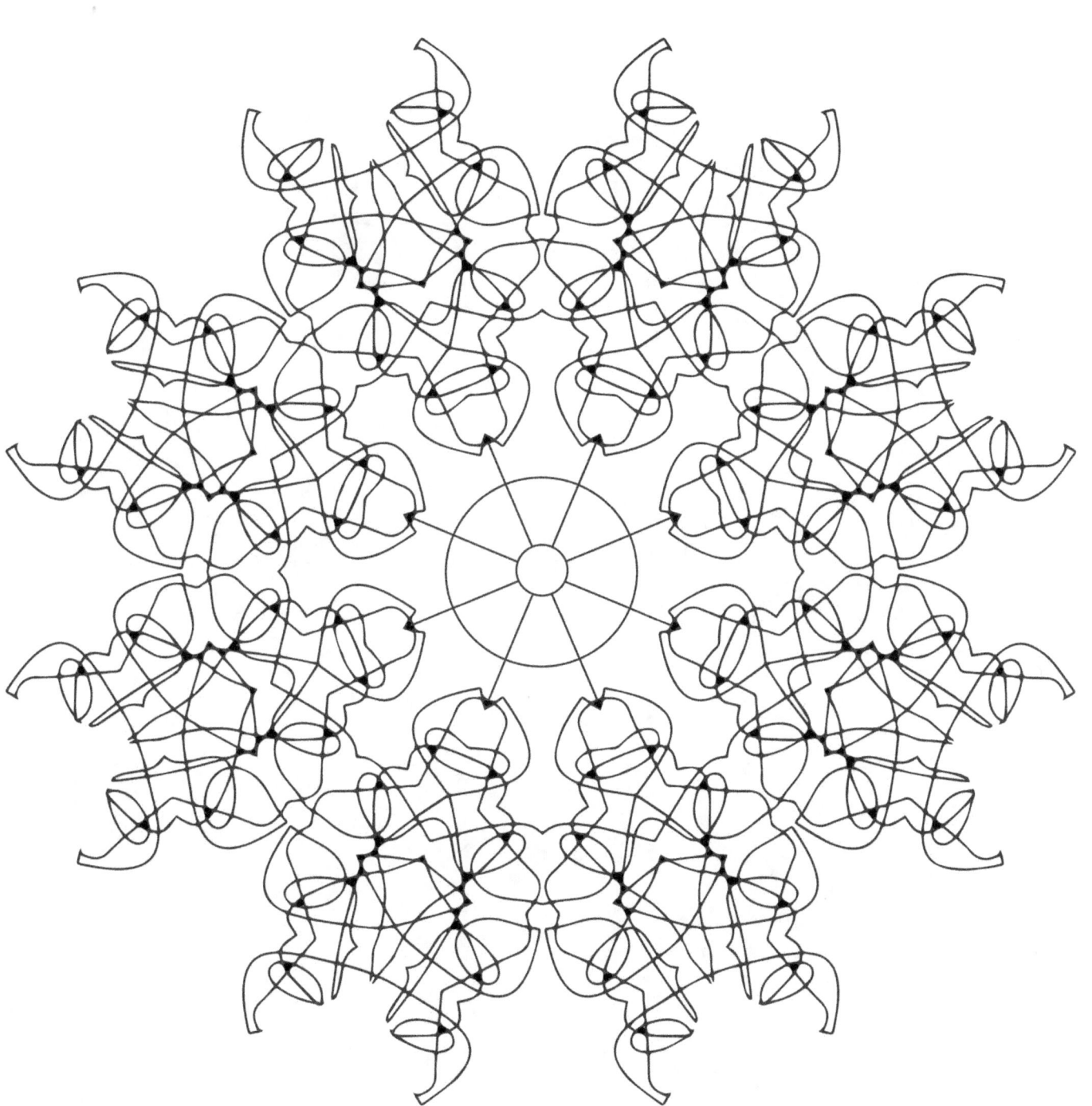

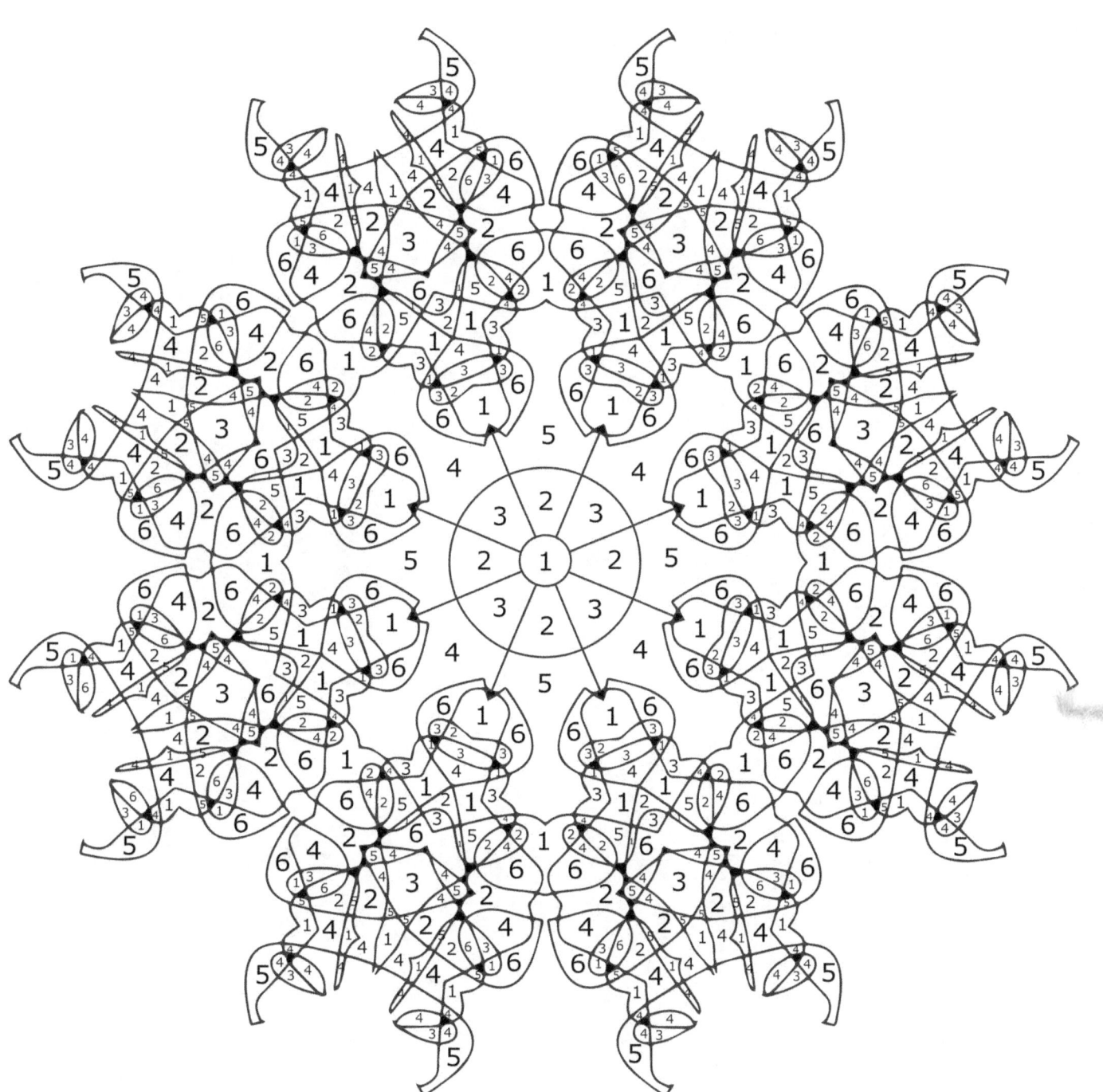

Suggested Colors:

1. Canary Yellow

2. Spanish Orange

3. Chartreuse

4. Poppy Red

5. Grass Green

6. Dark Green

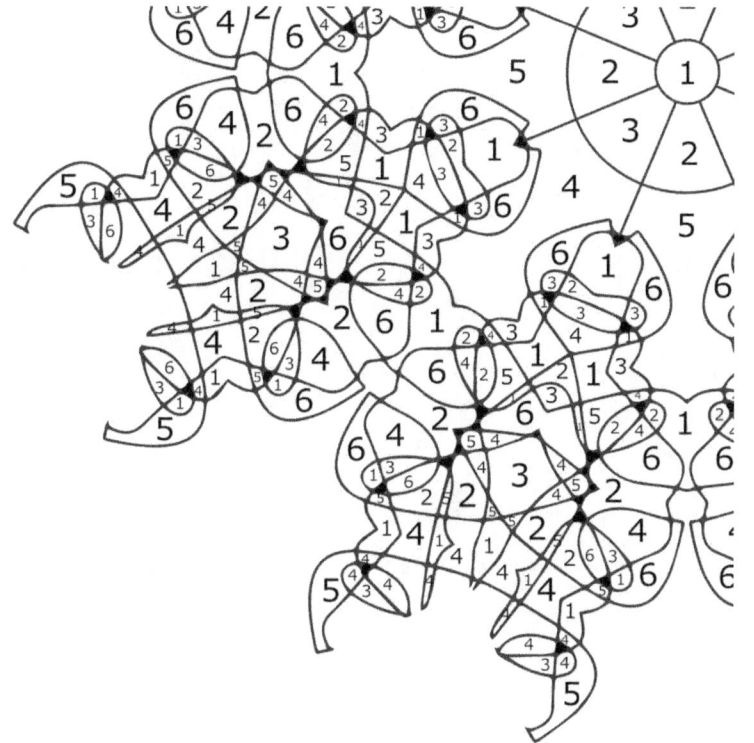

Test New Colors:

1.

2.

3.

4.

5.

6.

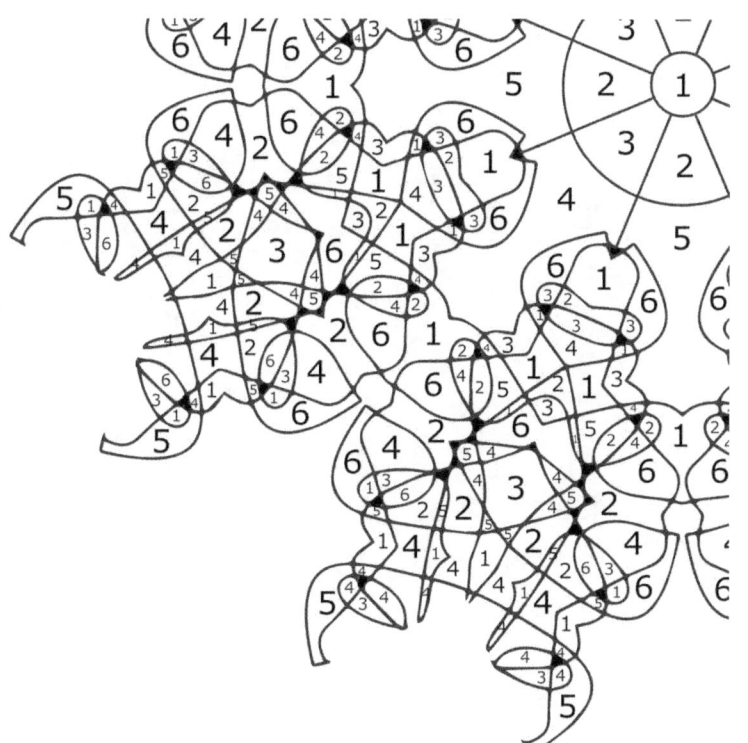

Test New Colors:

1.

2.

3.

4.

5.

6.

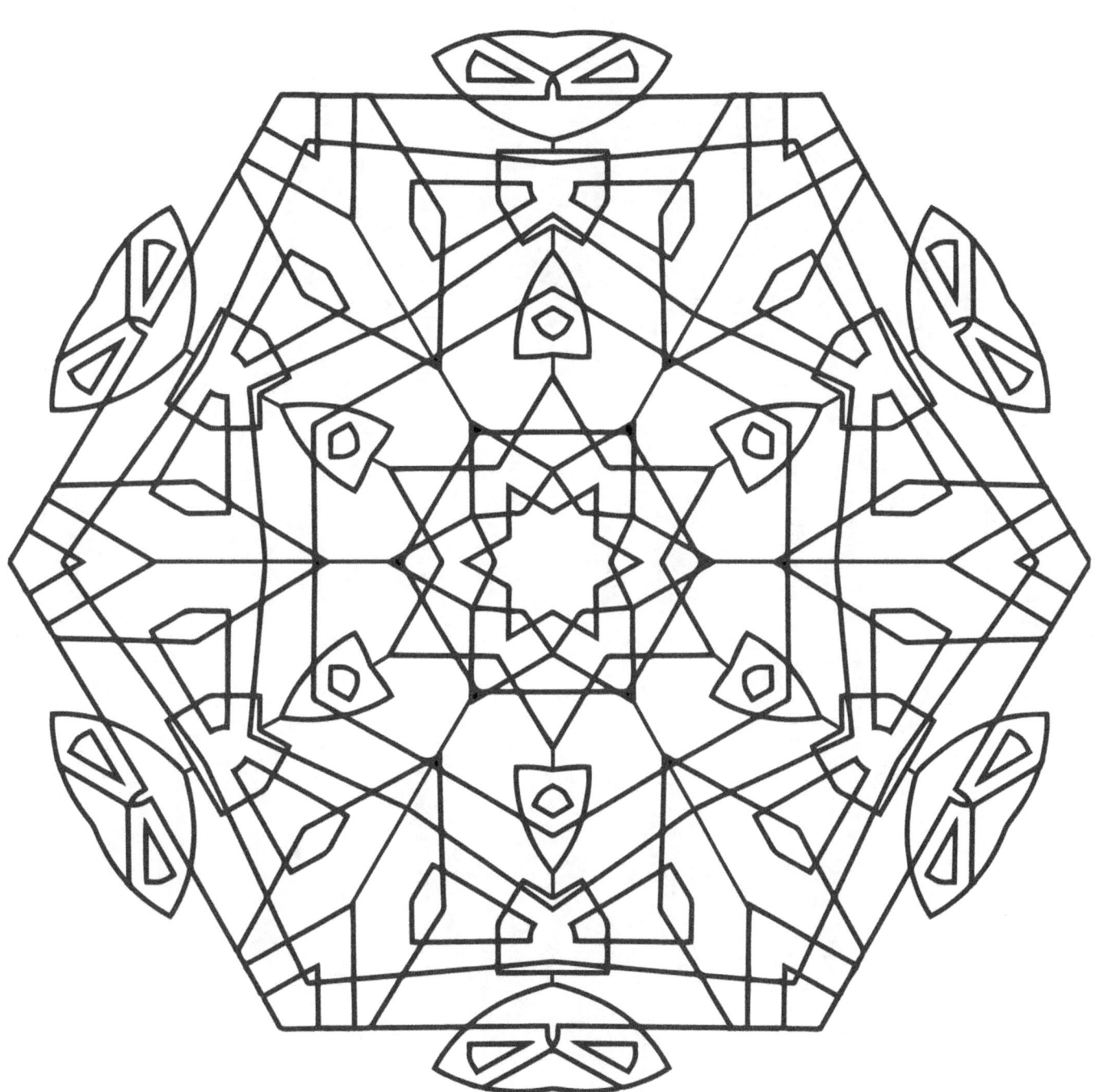

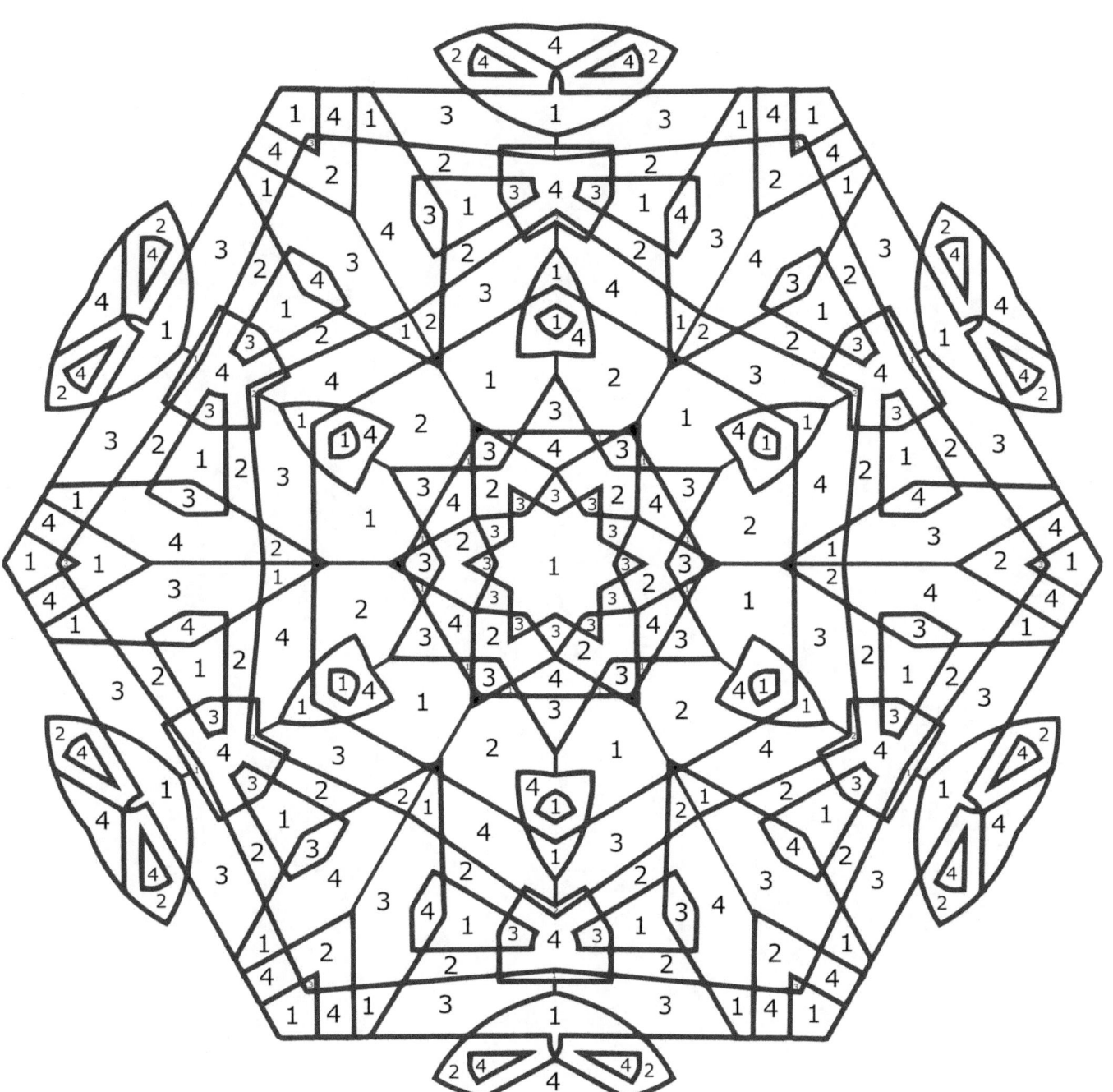

Suggested Colors:

1. Canary Yellow   4. Parma Violet

2. Scarlet Lake

3. Aquamarine

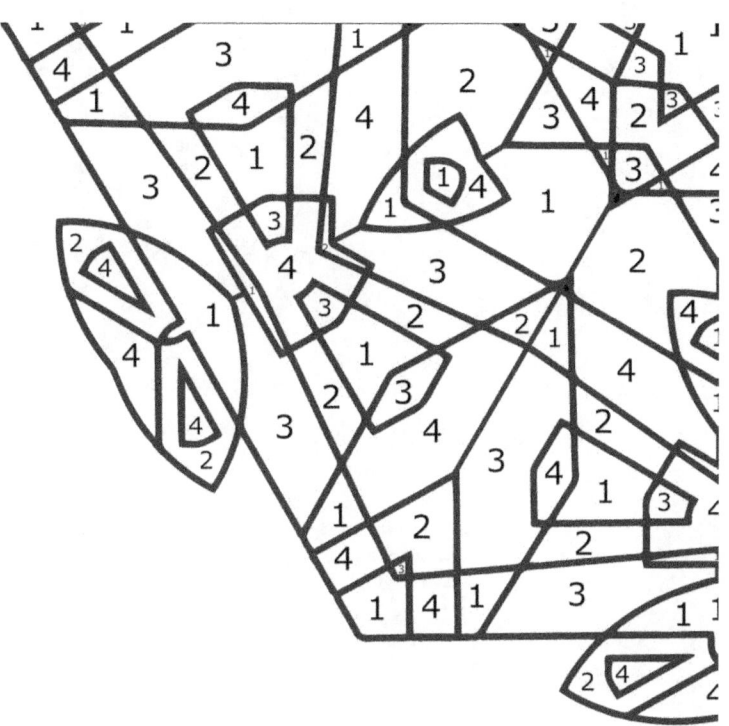

Test New Colors:

1.

2.

3.

4.

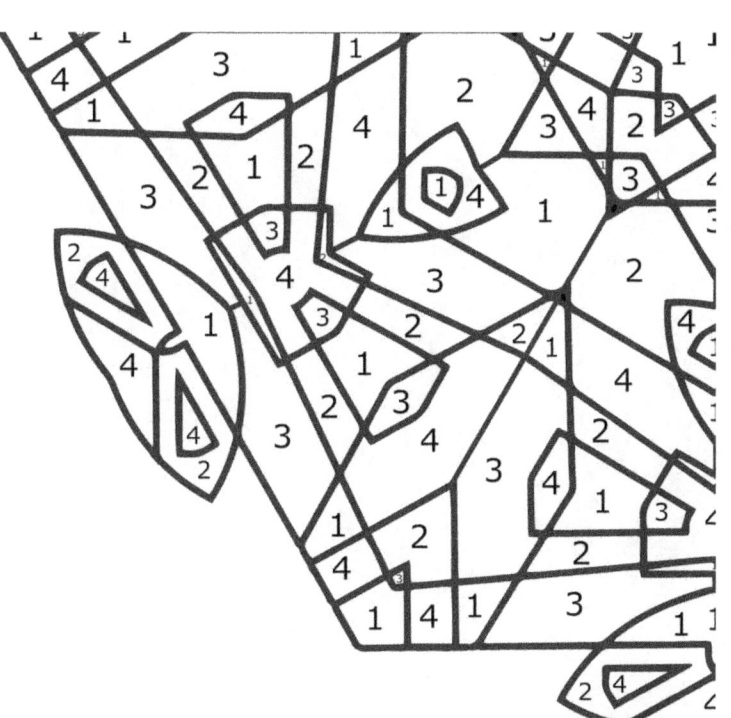

Test New Colors:

1.

2.

3.

4.

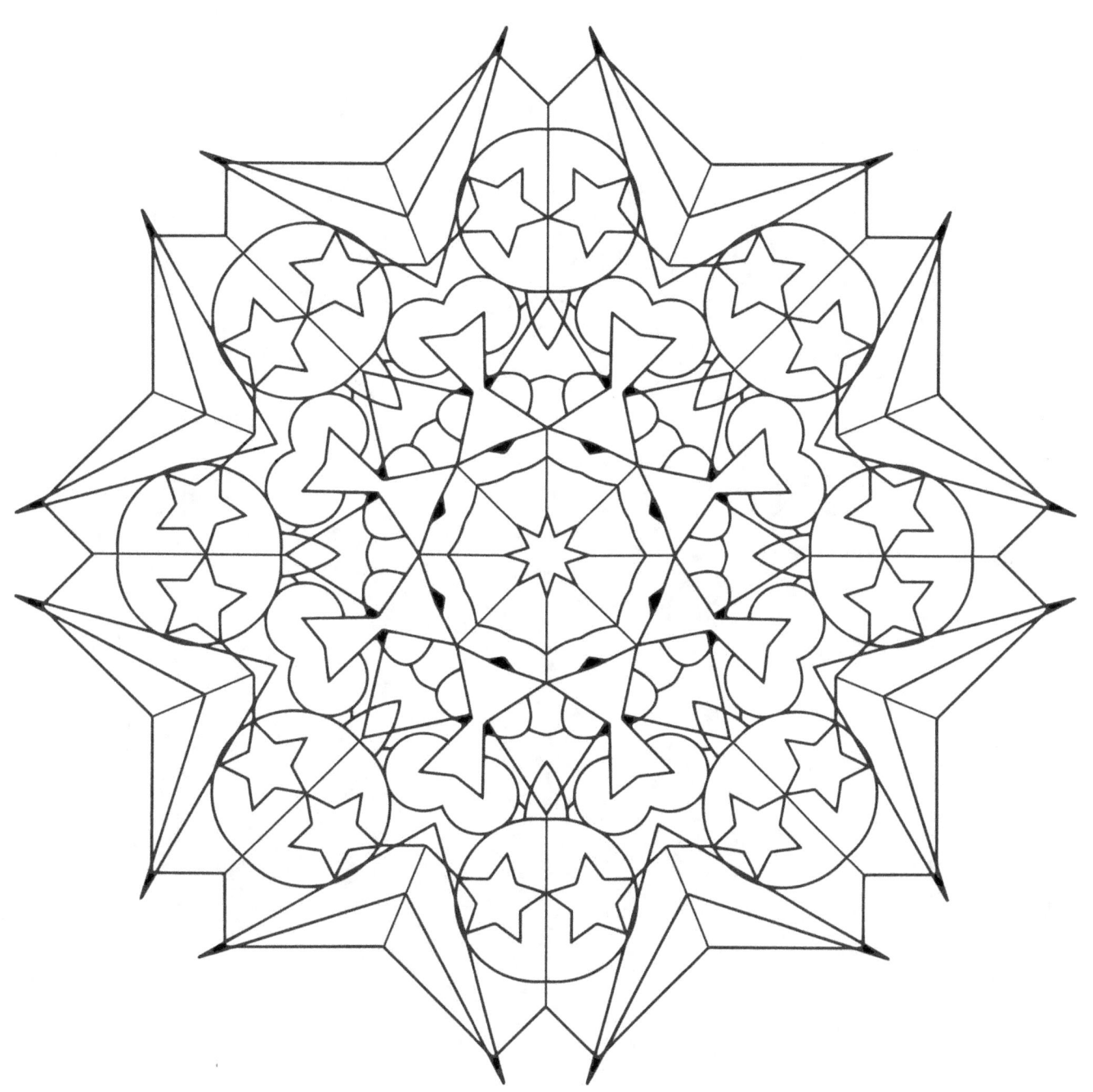

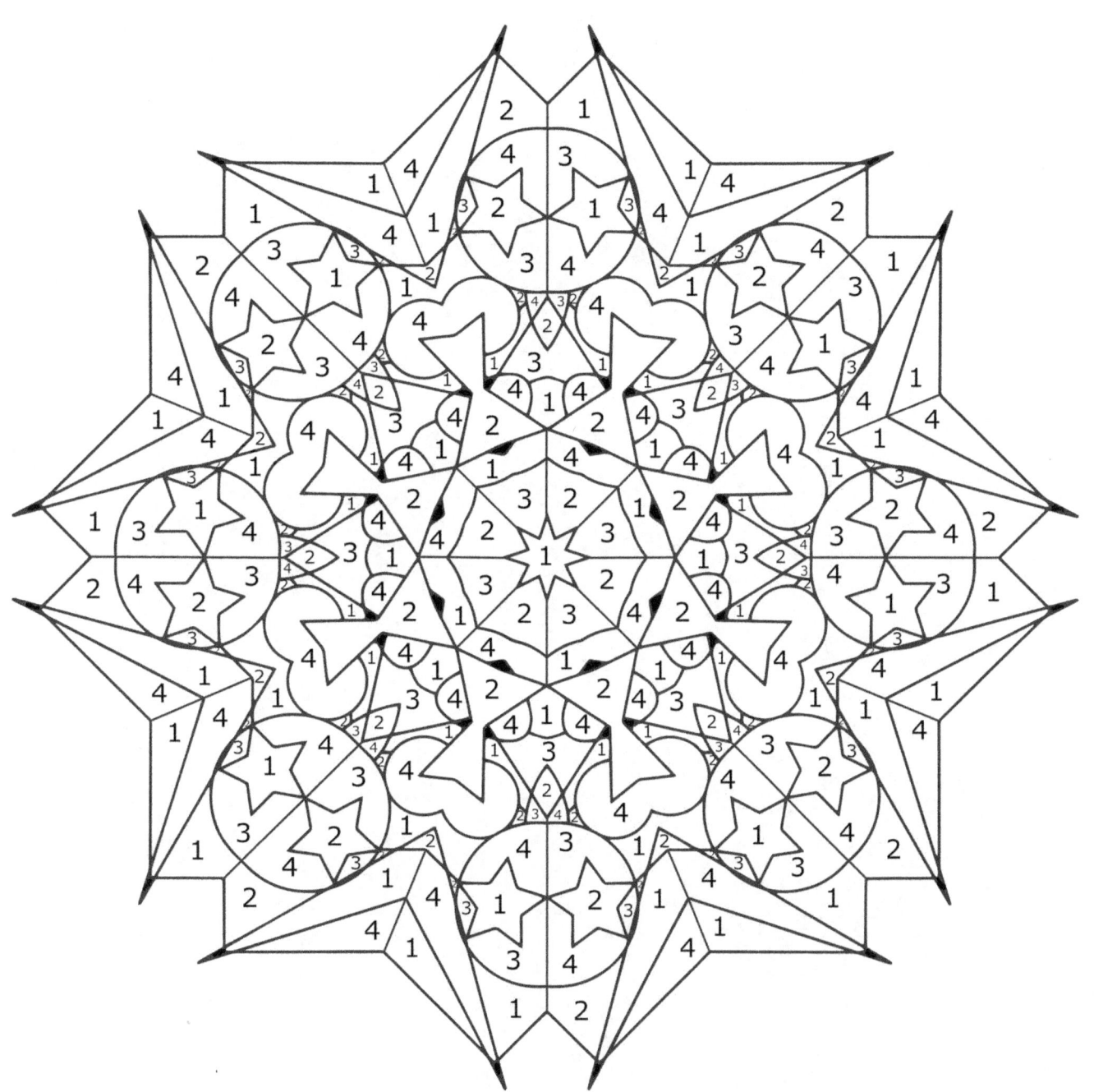

Suggested Colors:

1. Canary Yellow

2. Yellowed Orange

3. Process Red

4. Dahlia Purple

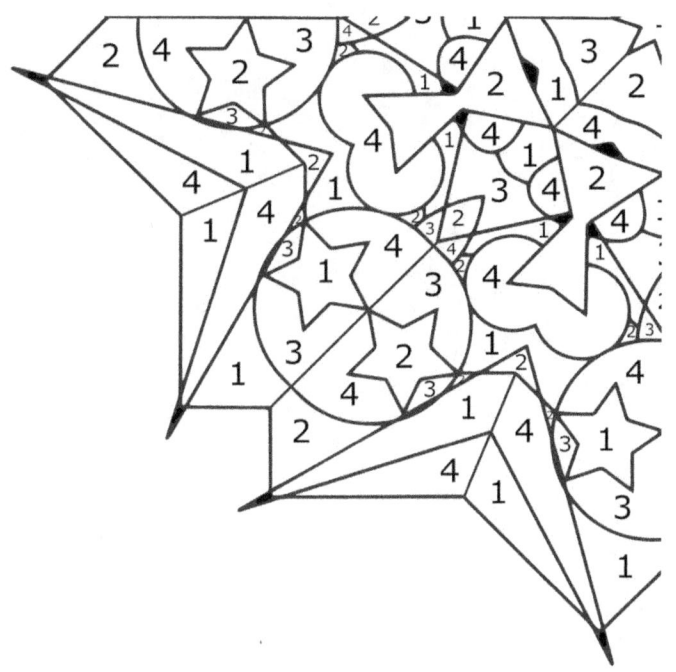

Test New Colors:

1.

2.

3.

4.

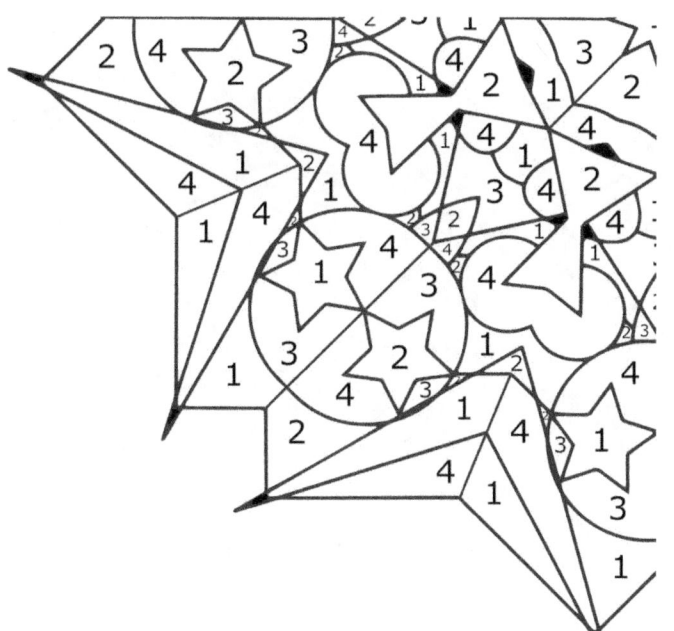

Test New Colors:

1.

2.

3.

4.

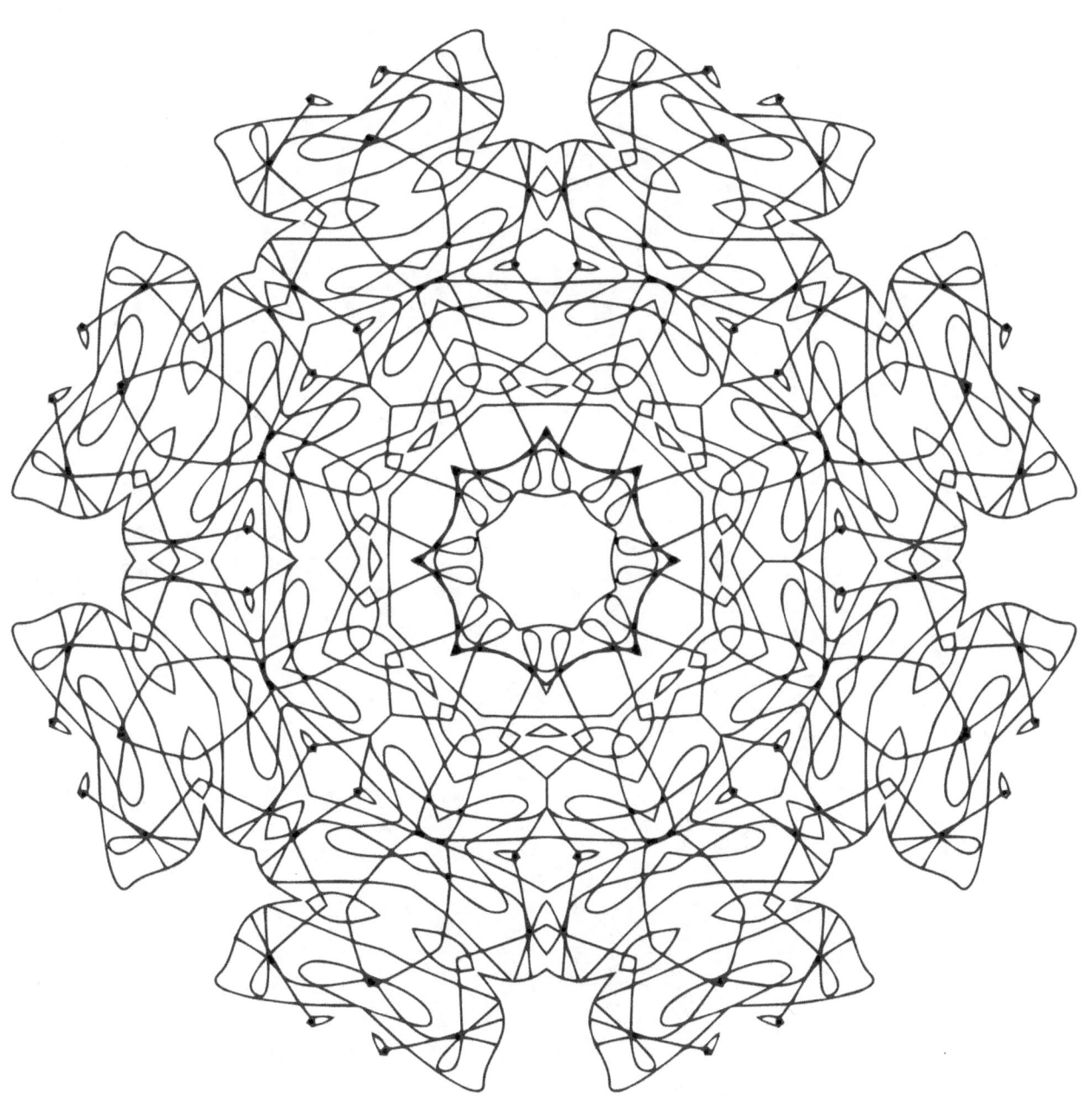

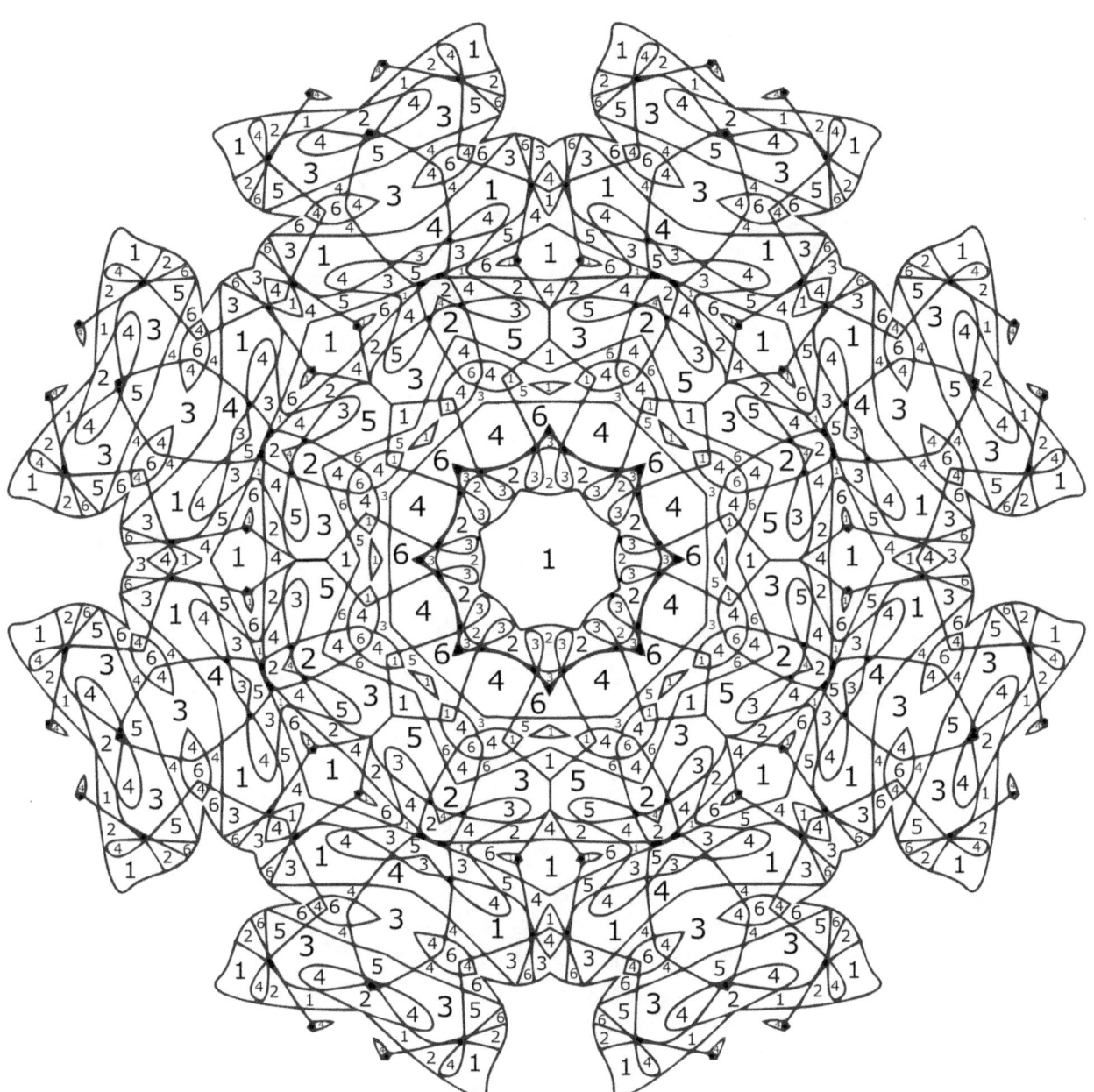

Suggested Colors:

1. Sunburst Yellow

2. Apple Green

3. Scarlet Lake

4. Magenta

5. Dahlia Purple

6. Electric Blue

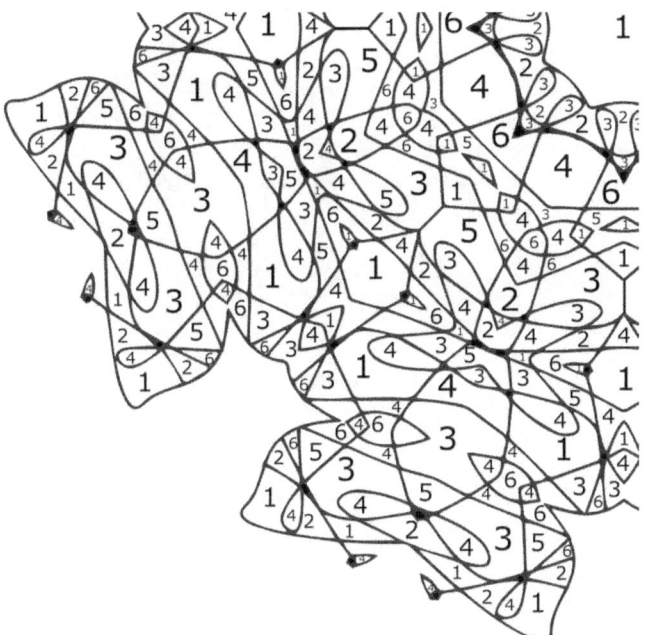

Test New Colors:

1.

2.

3.

4.

5.

6.

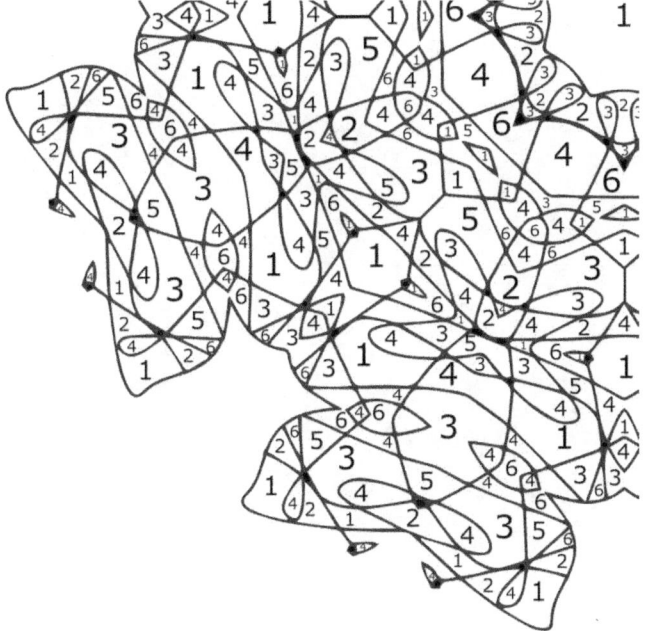

Test New Colors:

1.

2.

3.

4.

5.

6.

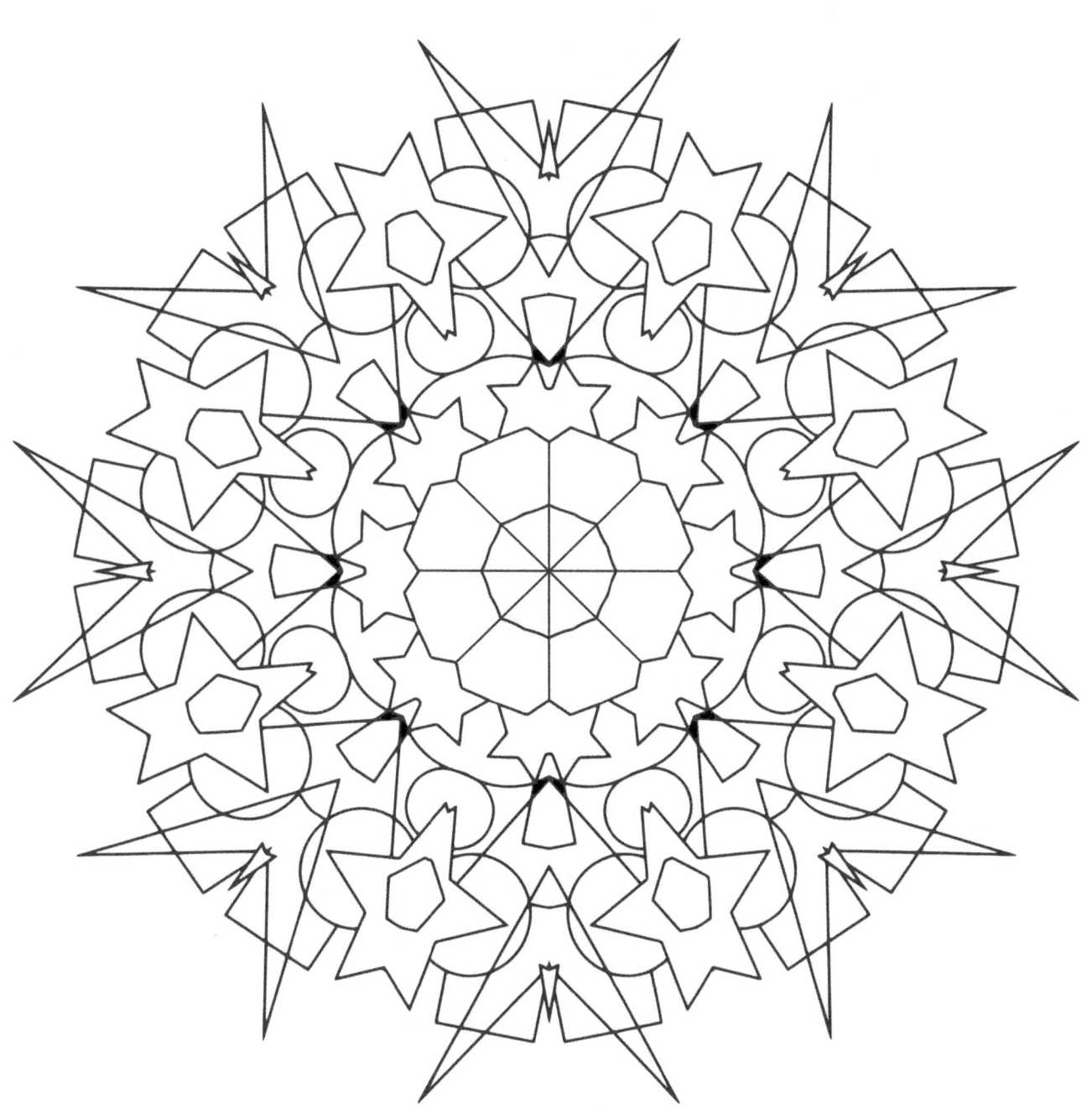

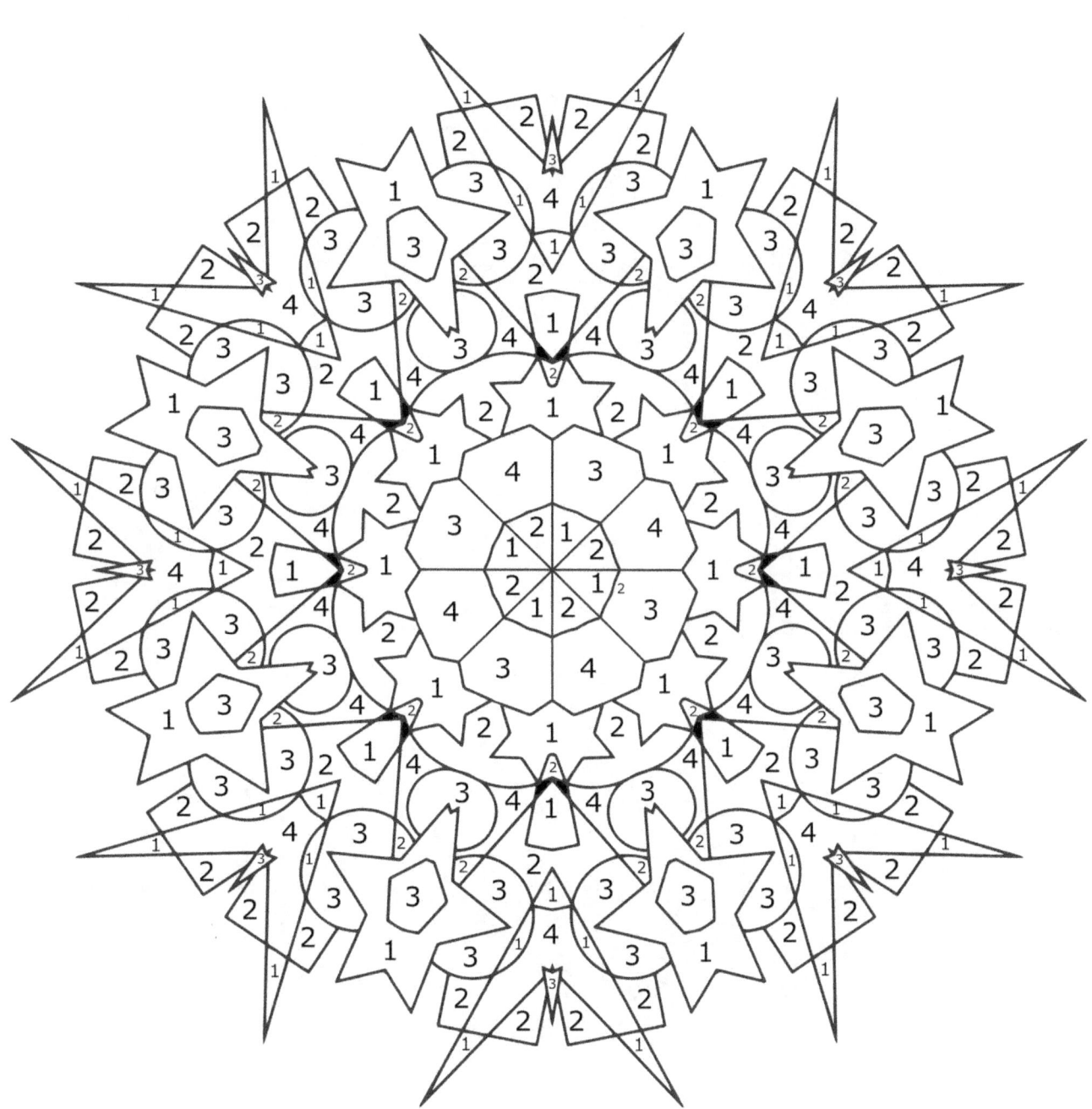

Suggested Colors:

1. Canary Yellow   4. Violet Blue

2. Spring Green

3. Aquamarine

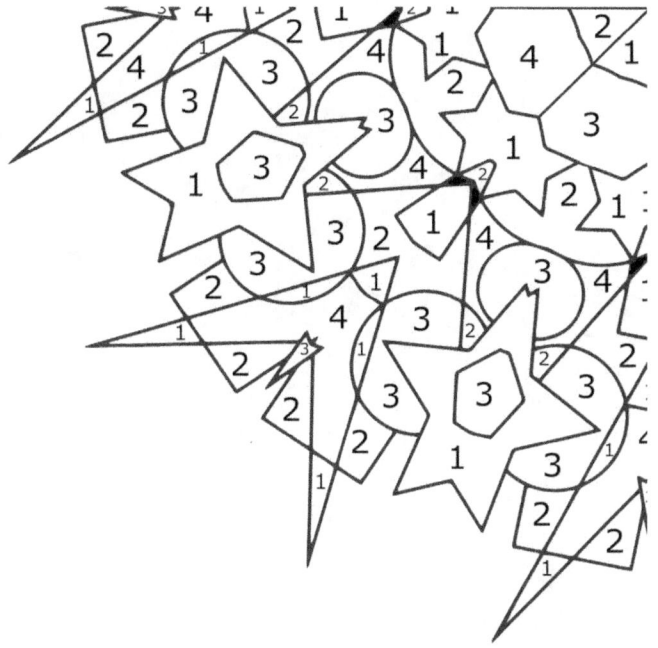

Test New Colors:

1.

2.

3.

4.

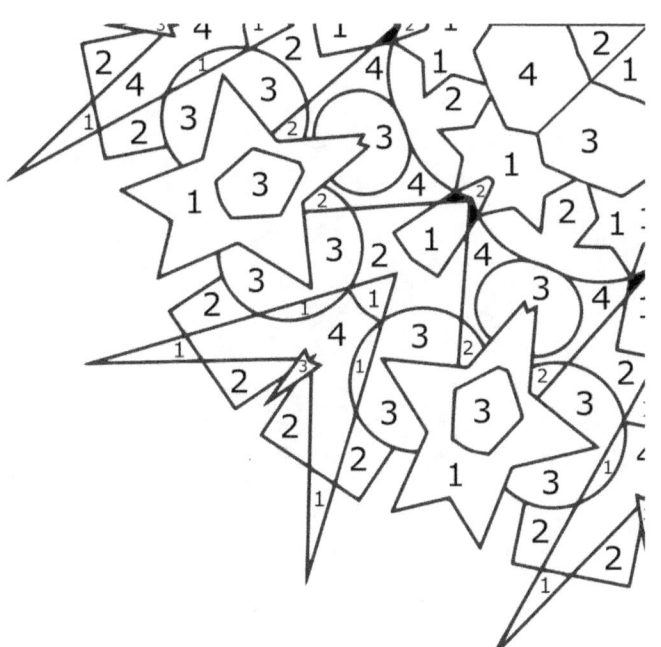

Test New Colors:

1.

2.

3.

4.

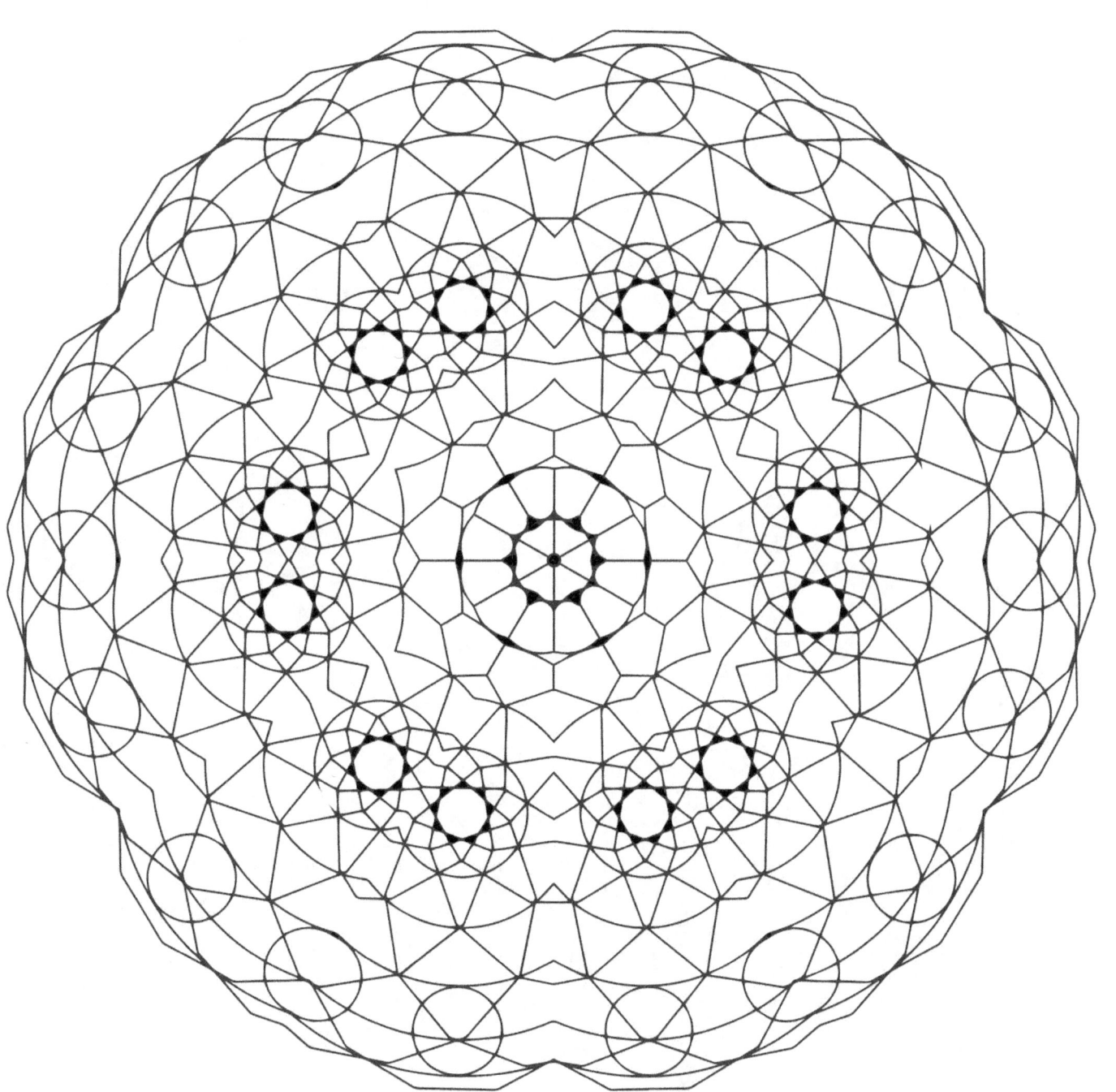

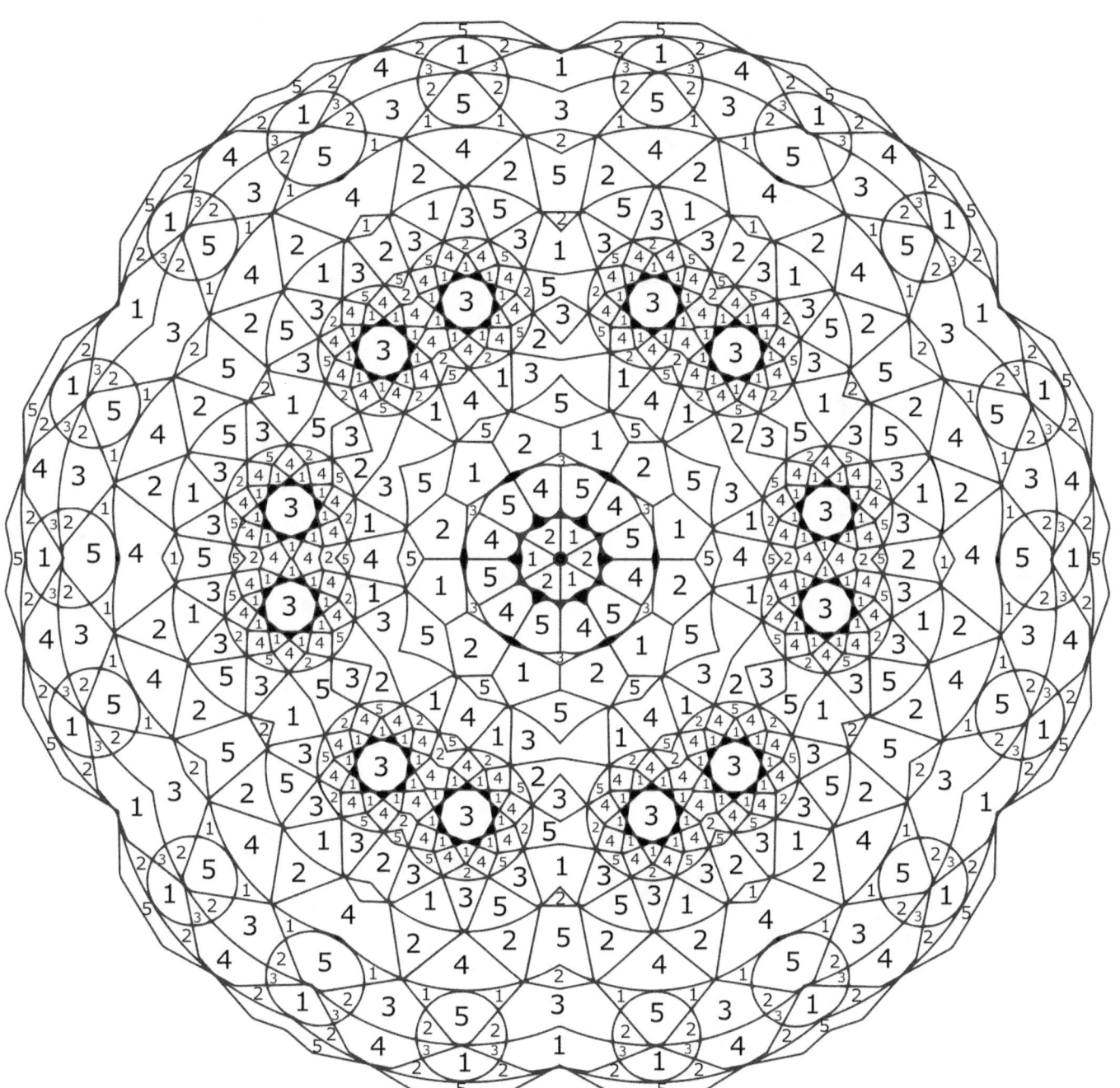

Suggested Colors:

1. Canary Yellow

4. Parma Violet

2. Spring Green

5. Light Cerulean Blue

3. Process Red

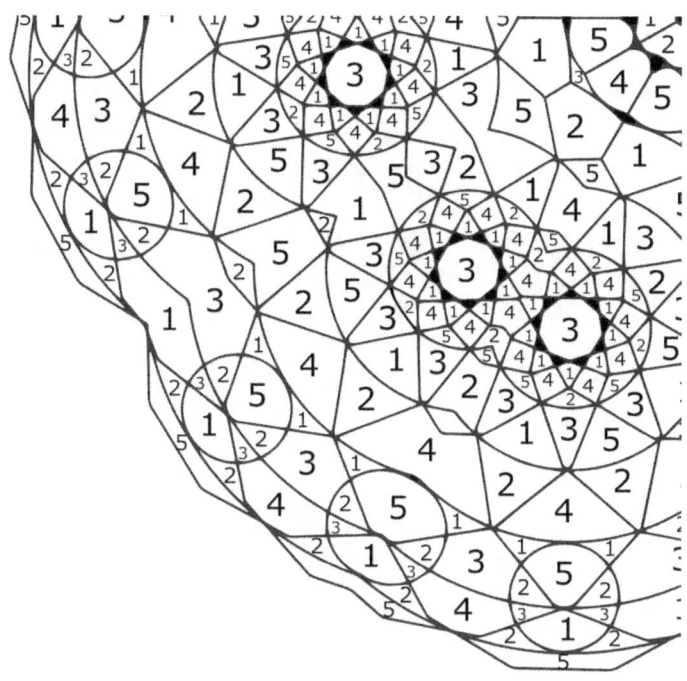

Test New Colors:

1.

2.

3.

4.

5.

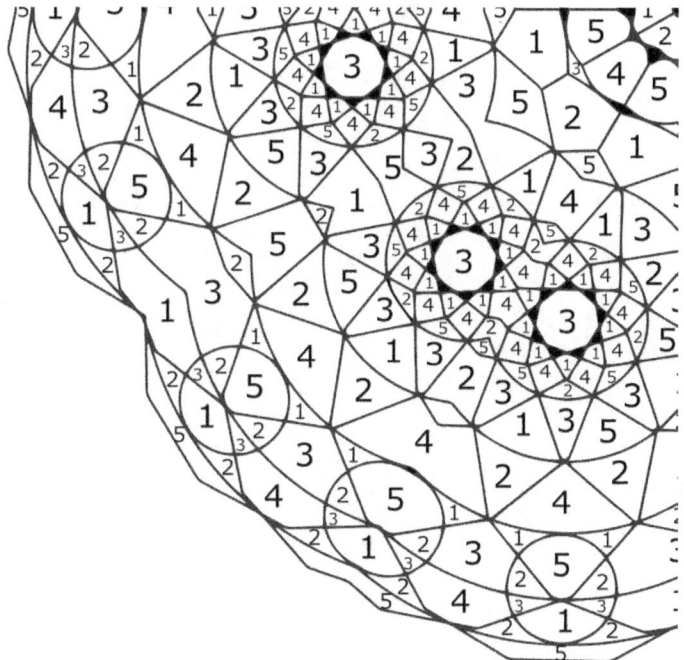

Test New Colors:

1.

2.

3.

4.

5.

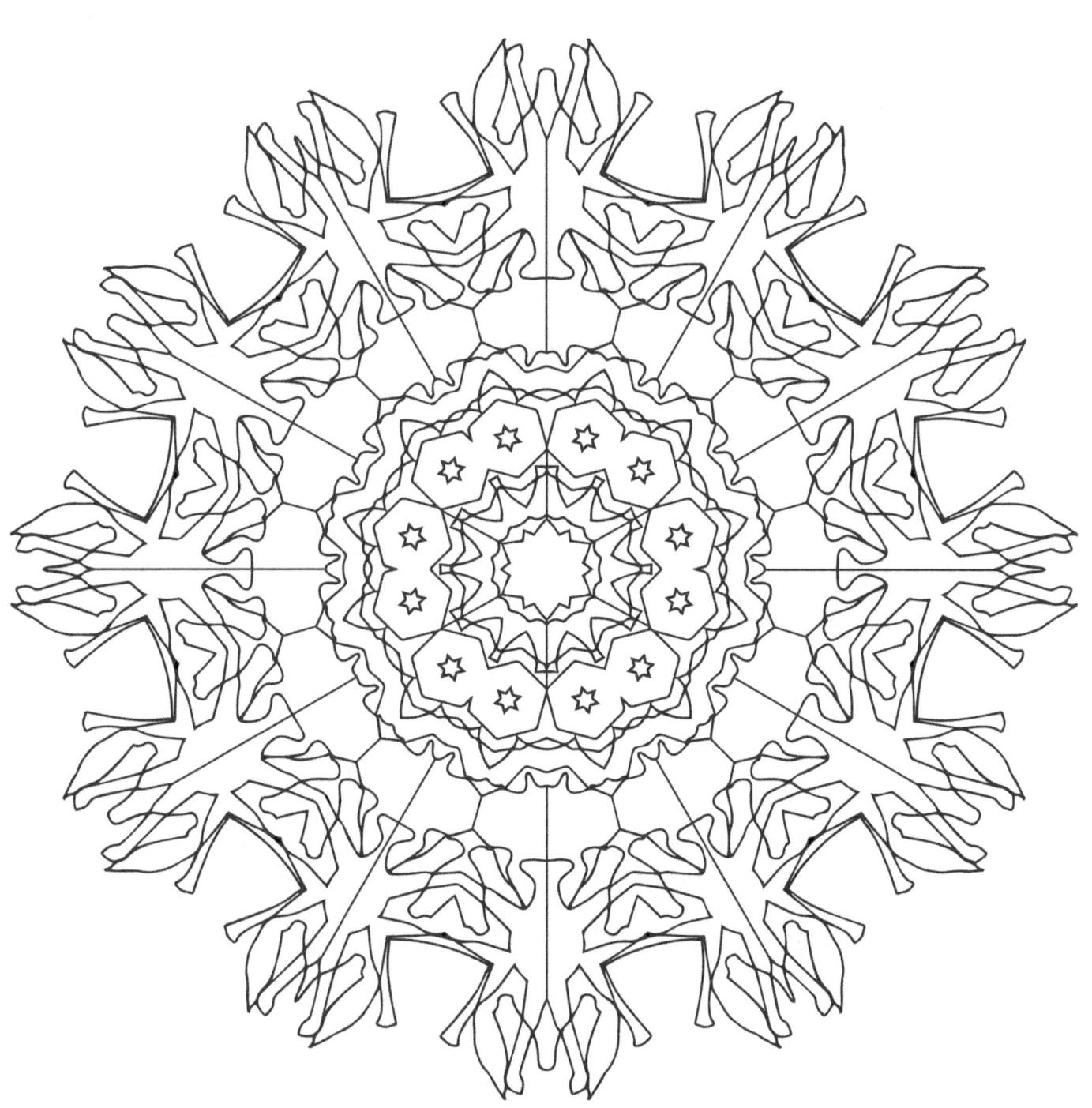

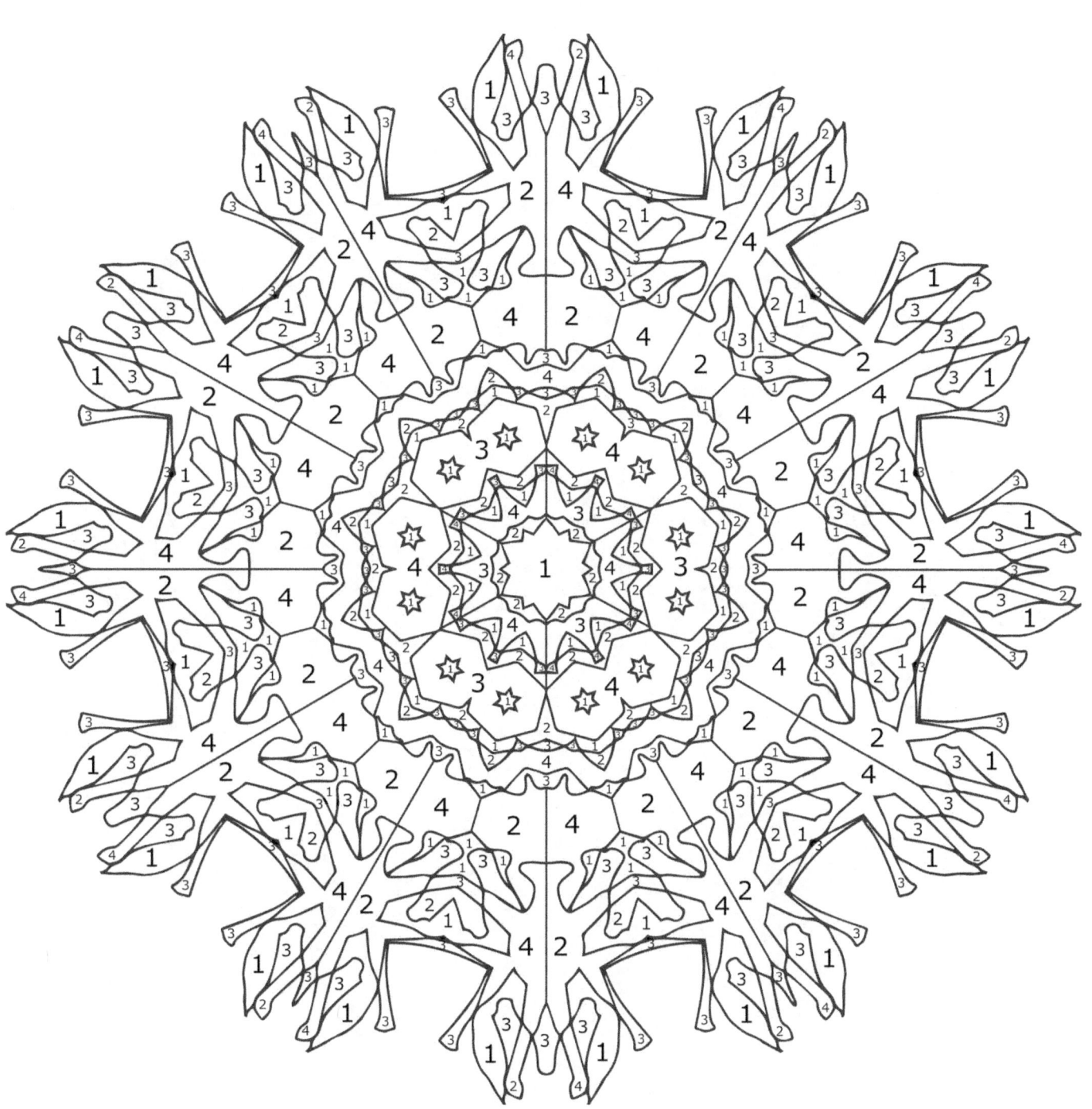

Suggested Colors:

1. Sunburst Yellow   4. Parma Violet

2. Yellowed Orange

3. Aquamarine

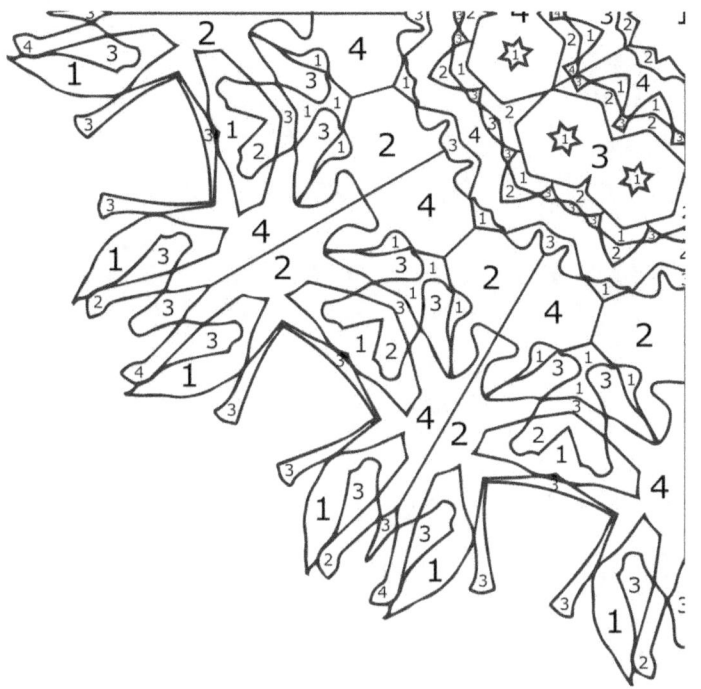

Test New Colors:

1.

2.

3.

4.

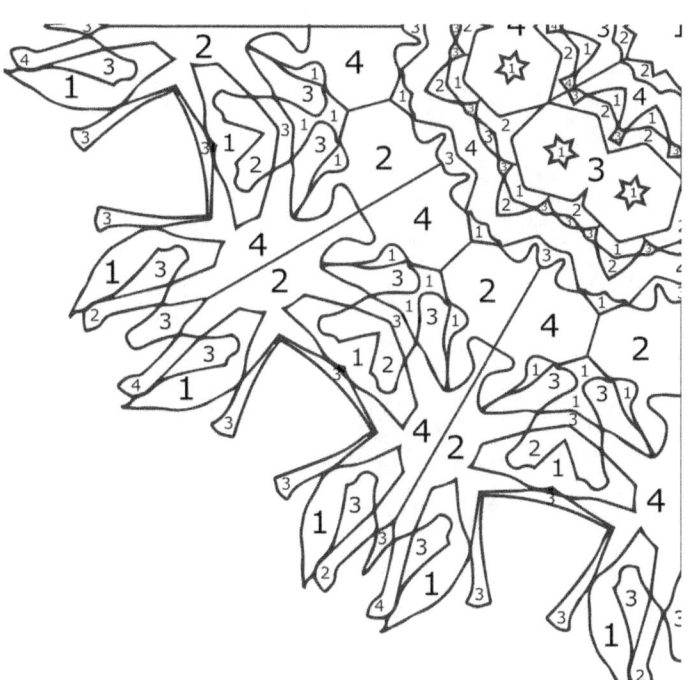

Test New Colors:

1.

2.

3.

4.

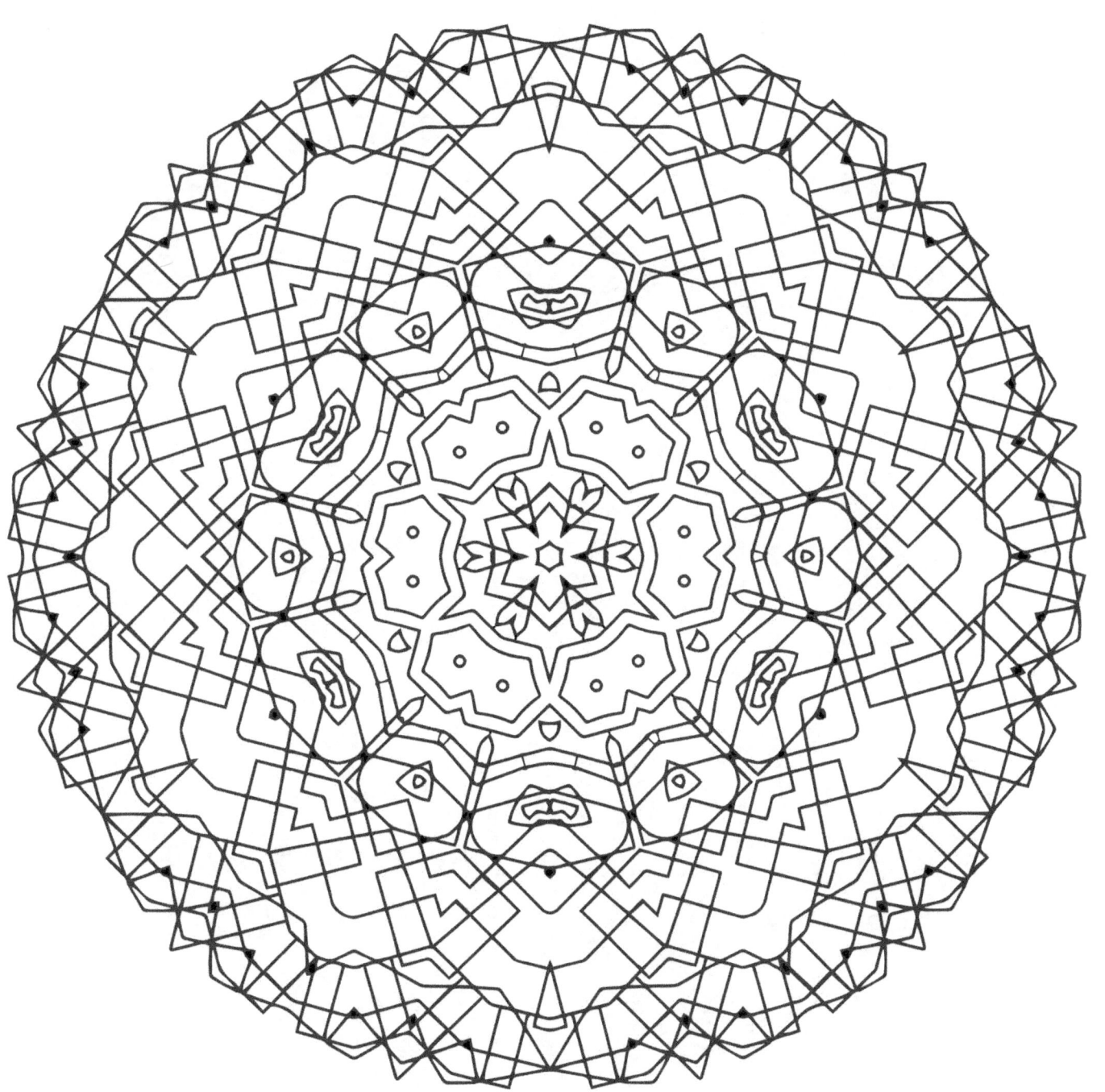

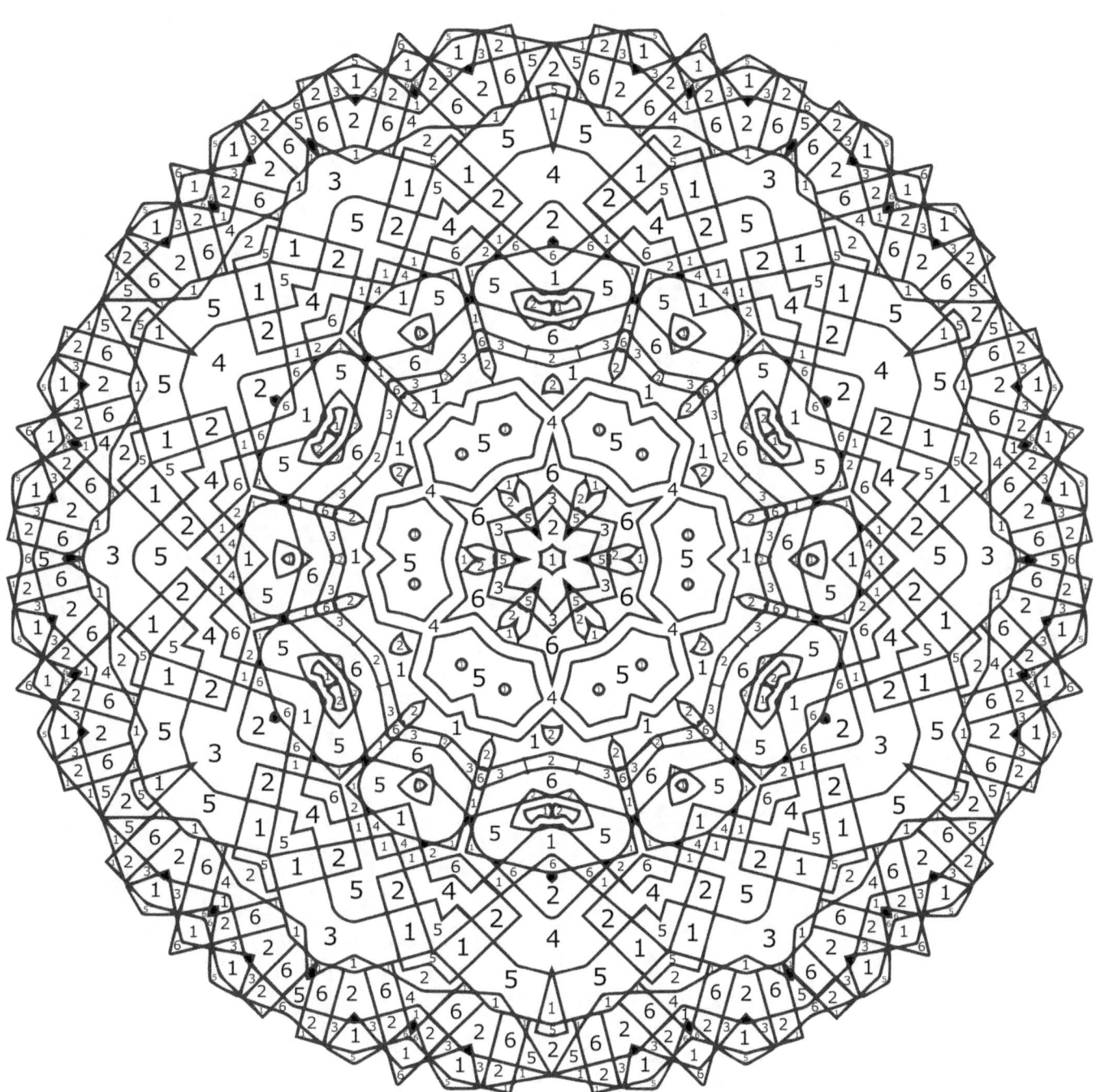

Suggested Colors:

1. Sunburst Yellow

2. Apple Green

3. Scarlet Lake

4. Magenta

5. Dahlia Purple

6. Electric Blue

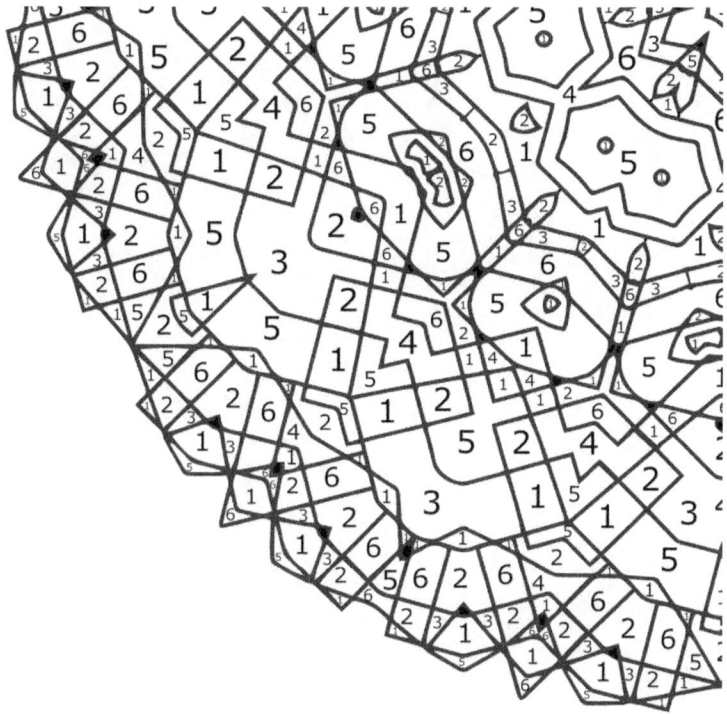

Test New Colors:

1.

2.

3.

4.

5.

6.

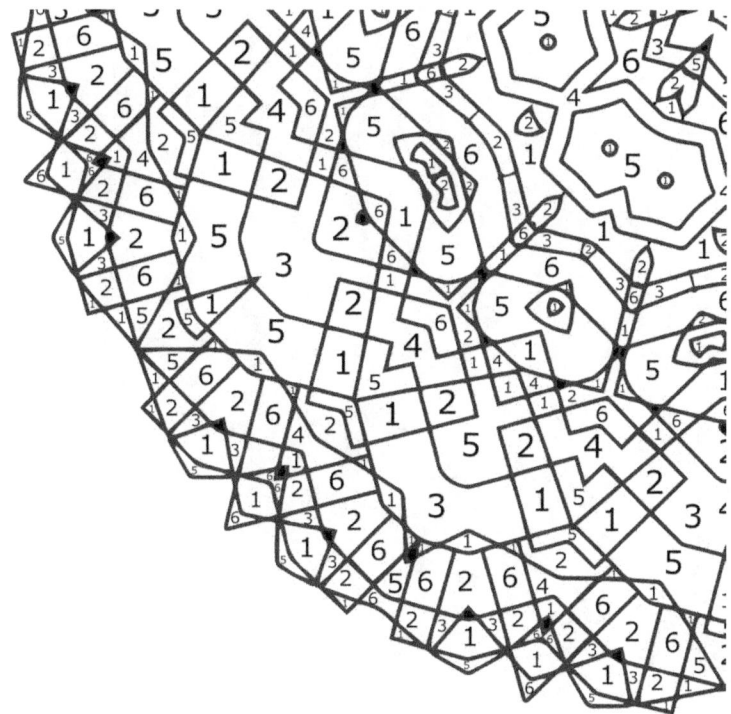

Test New Colors:

1.

2.

3.

4.

5.

6.

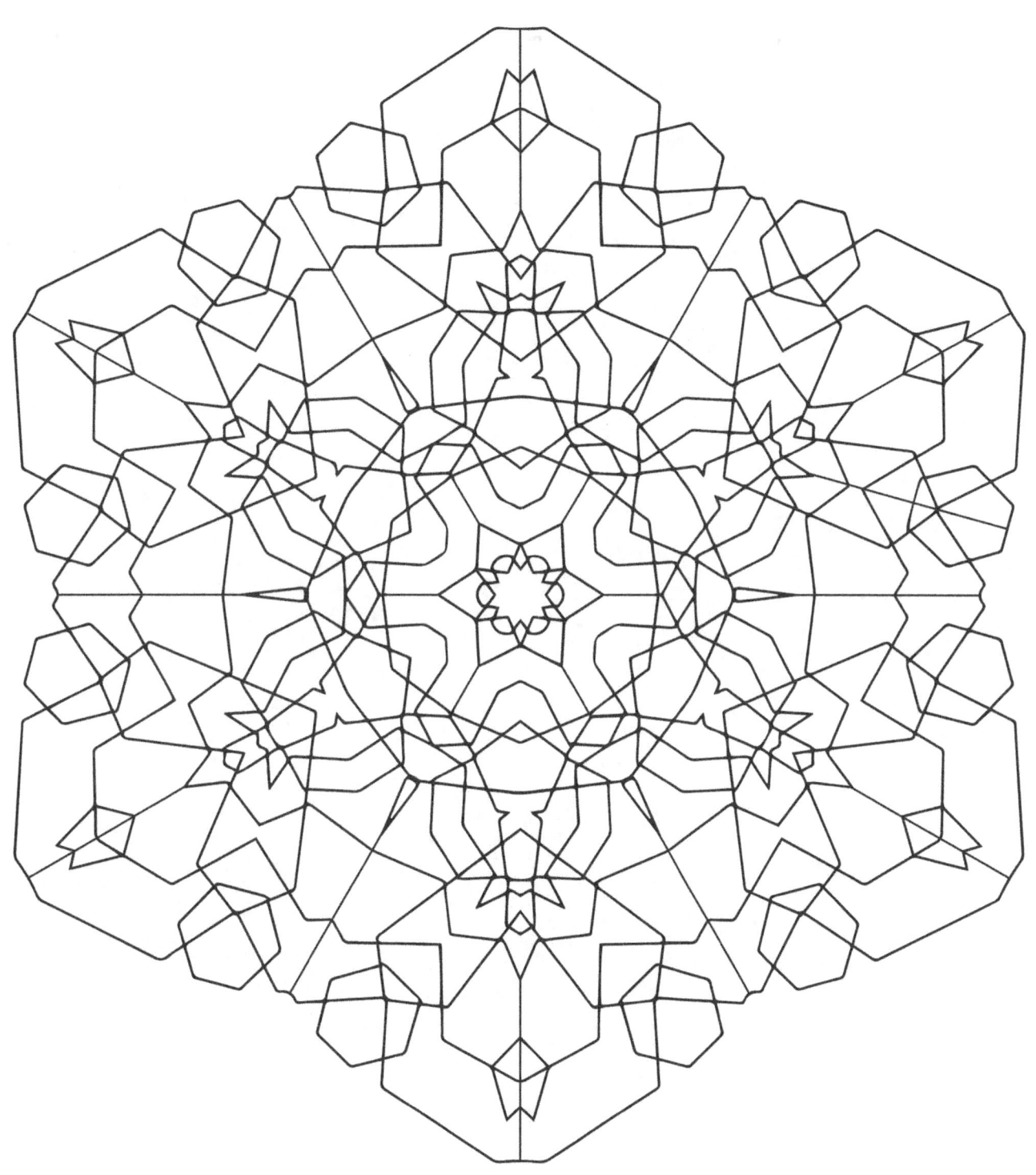

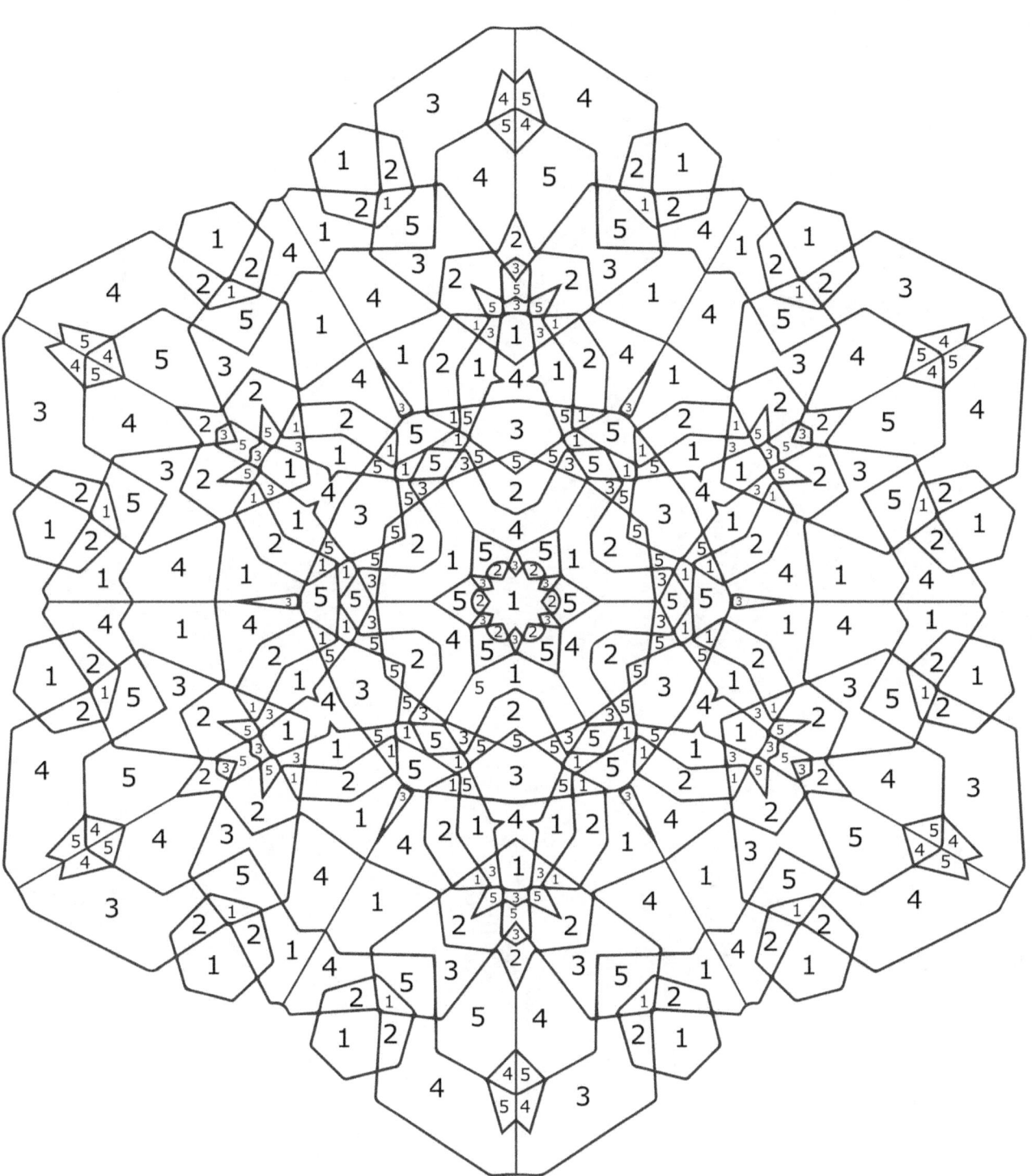

Suggested Colors:

1. Canary Yellow   4. Parma Violet

2. Spring Green   5. Light Cerulean

3. Process Red

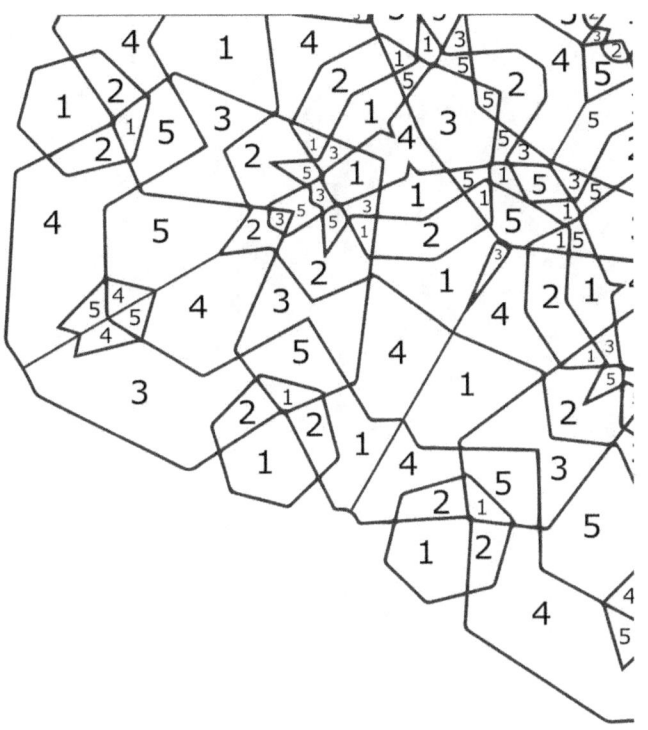

Test New Colors:

1.

2.

3.

4.

5.

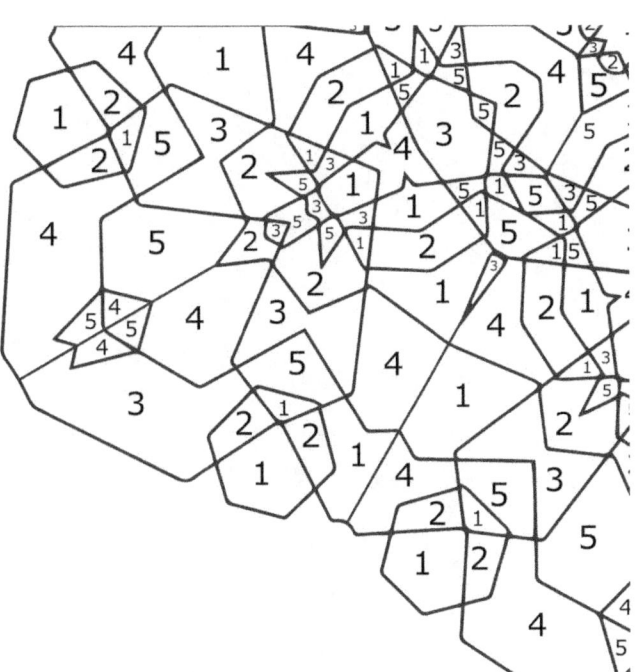

Test New Colors:

1.

2.

3.

4.

5.

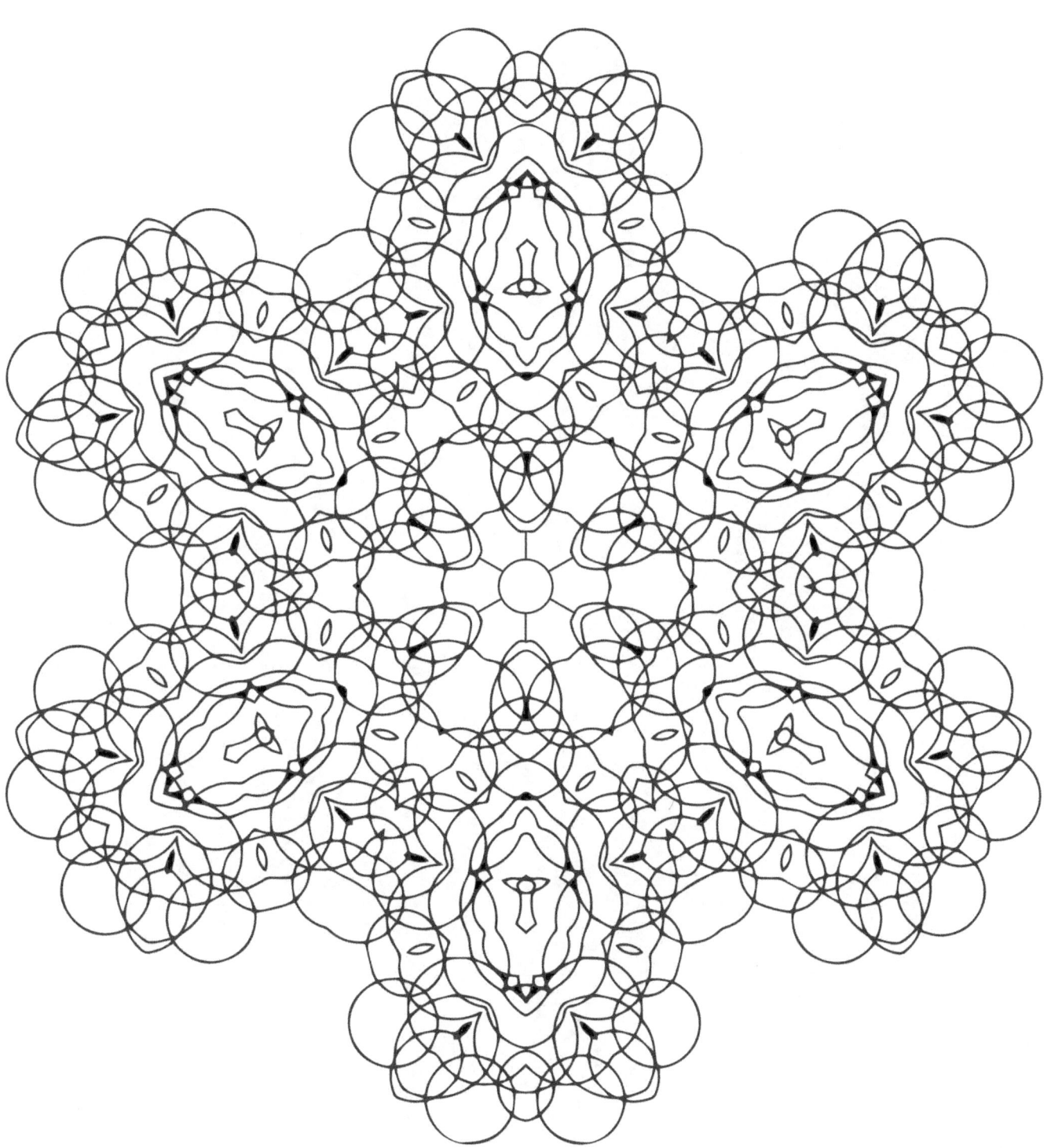

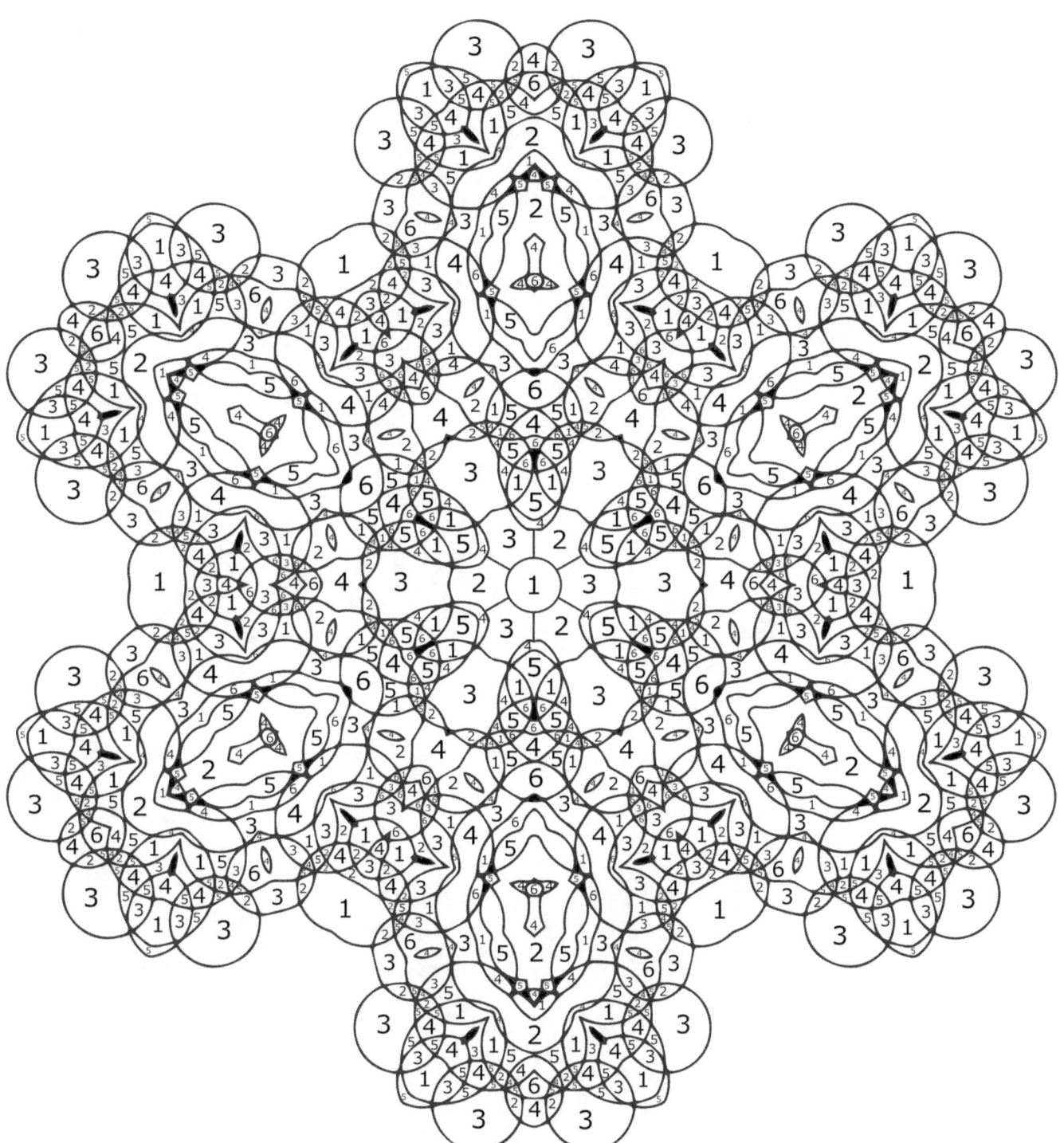

Suggested Colors:

1. Canary Yellow   4. Poppy Red

2. Spanish Orange   5. Grass Green

3. Chartreuse   6. Dark Green

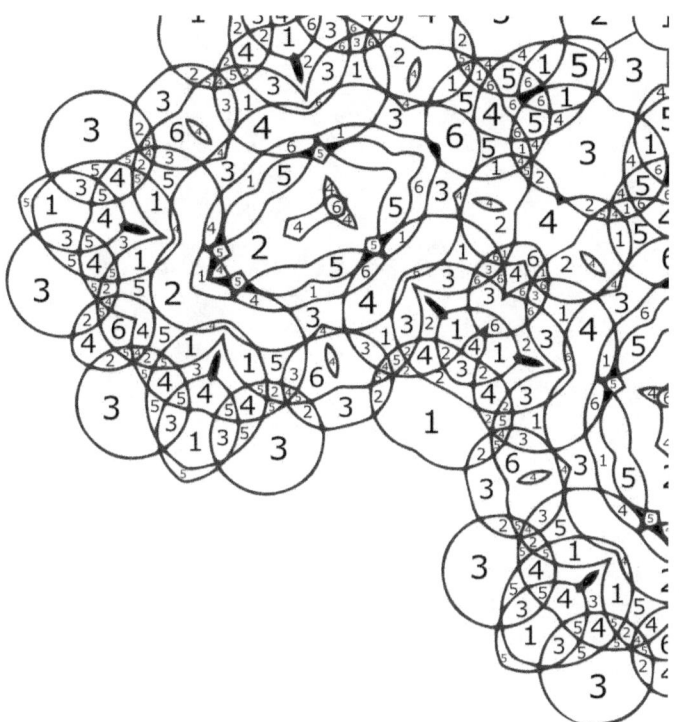

Test New Colors:

1.

2.

3.

4.

5.

6.

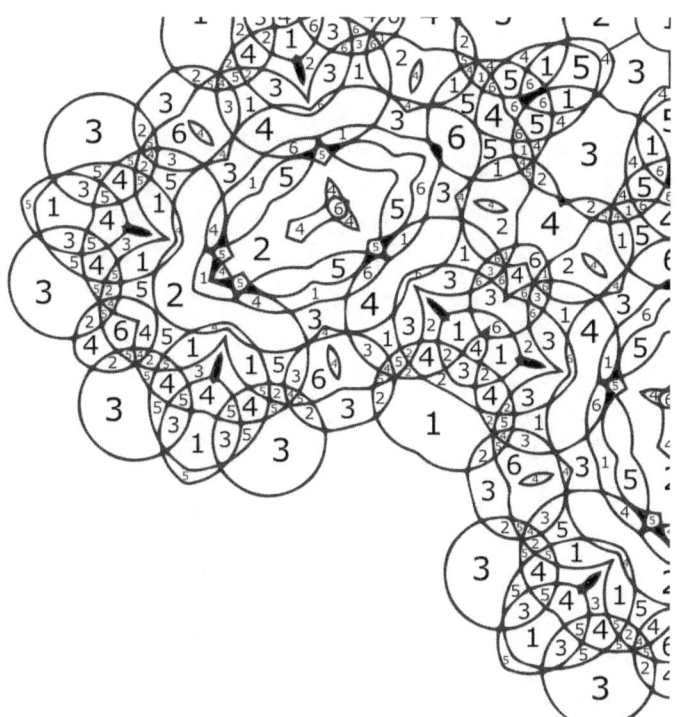

Test New Colors:

1.

2.

3.

4.

5.

6.

www.ingramcontent.com/pod-product-compliance
Lightning Source LLC
Chambersburg PA
CBHW080703190526

45169CB00006B/2219